WRECK AN OAST

Since 1803, when the first Cornish lifeboat was stationed at Penzance, a great humanitarian work of rescue from shipwreck has been carried on around the coast of the county with unfailing heroism and devotion by the men of this noble service.

The story of their work forms a magnificent saga, but one which has so far gone untold, and this history of the lifeboat service in Cornwall does belated justice to an undeservedly neglected subject. Based on official R.N.L.I. records, supplemented by information from local sources, it deals in detail with each of the Cornish stations past and present, together with a complete check list of rescues and services performed.

Books by the same authors

Cyril Noall

THE STORY OF THE ST. IVES LIFEBOATS

A HISTORY OF CORNISH MAIL- AND STAGE-COACHES

Grahame Farr

RECORDS OF BRISTOL SHIPS

CHEPSTOW SHIPS

SOMERSET HARBOURS

WEST COUNTRY PASSENGER STEAMERS

Wreck and Rescue Round the Cornish Coast

II. THE STORY OF THE LAND'S END LIFEBOATS

Cyril Noall and Grahame Farr

D. BRADFORD BARTON LTD
TRURO

First published 1965 by

D. BRADFORD BARTON LTD

TRURO BOOKSHOP TRURO CORNWALL

Printed by H. E. Warne Ltd St. Austell

CONTENTS

INTRODUCTION	7
ST. IVES	11
SENNEN COVE	46
ISLES OF SCILLY	69
PENZANCE-NEWLYN-PENLEE	106
PORTHLEVEN	142

ILLUSTRATIONS

The *Covent Garden* lifeboat of 1870-78, St Ives ..	33
The present St Ives lifeboat after a practice launch ..	33
The wreck of the brigantine *Julien Marie*, 1901 ..	34
Taking the crew off the Irish schooner *Loango*, 1909 ..	34
The minesweeper *H.M.S. Wave* ashore at St Ives, 1952 ..	51
The *Lizzie R. Wilce* and the *Mary Barrow*, St Ives, 1908 ..	51
The steamer *Alba* breaking up in rough seas, 1938 ..	52
The battered remains of the lifeboat *Caroline Parsons* ..	52
The funeral pyre of the *John and Sarah Eliza Stych* ..	53
The s.s. *Bessemer City* on Pen Enys Point, 1936 ..	53
The schooner *Mildred* half-submerged, Gurnard's Head, 1912	54

ILLUSTRATIONS

The full-rigged ship *Alexander Yeats*, Gurnard's Head, 1896 54
The Italian steamer *Aida Lauro* near Botallack, 1937 .. 71
The s.s. *Malta* wrecked south of Botallack, 1889 .. 71
The collier *Datetree* wrecked on The Brisons, 1914 .. 72
H.M. Submarine *L.I.* ashore at Cape Cornwall .. 72
The wreck of the s.s. *Ixia*, St Just, 1929 72
The Cardiff steamer *Blue Jacket* on the Longships, 1898 73
Sennen Cove lifeboat *The Newbons* returning from a mission 73
The wreck of the barque *Trifolium* at Sennen, 1914 .. 74
The ship *Horsa* aground off St Martin's, Scilly, 1893 .. 91
The liner *Minnehaha* ashore on Bryher, Scilly, 1910 .. 92
The St Agnes lifeboat pulling to the *Ardencraig*, 1911 .. 92
The s.s. *Castleford* on the Western Rocks, Scilly, 1887 .. 93
The St Mary's lifeboat towing off the *Lord Haldane*, 1929 93
The collier *Llandaff* ashore near Land's End, 1889 .. 94
The s.s. *Wimborne* wrecked at Carn Barra Point, 1910 .. 94
The coaster *Falmouth Castle* beached near Porthcurno, 1919 111
Rescue by breeches-buoy from the s.s. *City of Cardiff*, 1912 111
The *Granite State* ashore at Porthcurno, 1895 .. 112
Salvage work on the s.s. *Cragoswald*, Mousehole, 1911 .. 112
Six Cornish lifeboats racing in Mount's Bay in 1867 .. 113
The Penzance lifeboat launching to the *Jeune Hortense*, 1888 113
The brigantine *Henry Harvey* stranded off Penzance, 1898 114
The wreck of the barque *Petrellen* near Marazion, 1885 114
The barque *Saluto* drifting shorewards east of Marazion, 1911 131
The barque *Noisiel* ashore at Praa Sands, 1905 .. 131
The s.s. *Tripolitania* flung high onto Loe Bar, Porthleven, 1912 132

INTRODUCTION

THIS SECOND volume in the story of wreck and rescue on the Cornish coast covers the 'toe' of Cornwall and the Isles of Scilly. Rugged granite cliffs keep back the sea from Penwith—the old Cornish name for this peninsula—with only here and there a cove. In fact, from St. Ives Bay, round the land to Mount's Bay, there is only one considerable beach, that at Whitesand Bay, Sennen. The Isles of Scilly lie 28 miles out on the fringe of the Atlantic, mysterious and somehow spell-binding. They are visible on clear days from Land's End, where one looks out over the site of the land of Lyonesse, swallowed by the sea many centuries ago. Today five of the Islands are inhabited, perhaps forty more are large enough to be grass-bearing, but in addition there are countless rocks, some isolated, and some in clusters.

The Islands and the uncompromising bastion of the mainland take the full force of westerly gales sweeping in from the ocean, and between them they probably account for the greater number of the wrecks which have occurred on all the coasts of Cornwall. In ancient times seaborne goods were unshipped and carried overland from Hayle to Marazion, rather than compel the frail ships to face the unpredictable winds and seas off Land's End. Throughout the days of sail the area was one to be passed as quickly as possible, and the slightest indication of a strong blow would send craft of all sizes from smacks to full-rigged ships running for shelter into St. Ives or Mount's Bays. Their safety would depend upon how good was their tackle and their knowledge of the holding properties of the sea bottom. Even when riding in apparent safety, the situation could, and frequently did, change in a few minutes by a shift of wind. If from westerly it became more northerly, St. Ives Bay could become a death trap; if more southerly the same would apply to Mount's Bay, and the leeward beaches would lie with the surf thundering on to them, waiting for some hapless vessel with an anchor chain that failed the supreme test.

Mount's Bay at one end of that great east-west traffic lane, the English Channel, was the busier of the two anchorages. Here was the first lifeboat of the Duchy, purchased by local subscriptions and a generous grant from Lloyd's, in 1803. Short-lived though this lifeboat was, as will be seen later, Penzance again had the first lifeboat at the revival which followed the formation, in 1824, of the National Institution for the Preservation of Life from Shipwreck, father of the Royal National Life-boat Institution.

Although the Isles of Scilly received a lifeboat in 1837, and St. Ives one in 1840, by 1850 the national service had again entered the doldrums. The Northumberland Report of 1851, which, *inter alia*, reviewed the state existing in the country's life-saving services, remarked—"From Falmouth, round the Land's End, by Trevose Head to Hartland Point, an extent of 150 miles of the most exposed coast in England, there is not a really efficient lifeboat." And *The Times* was constrained to elaborate this finding with some forthright criticism—

"The Duke of Cornwall is still a minor, but he mounts a blue jacket and tarpaulin truck, and is of an age to pity and feel for the shipwrecked seaman, if his case is only properly placed before him. Is it fitting that the Prince of Wales should be surpassed in munificence by any of his future subjects, albeit a Duke of Northumberland—nay, is it fitting that the country squires of Norfolk and Suffolk, and the burgesses of their several sea-coast towns, should keep up an efficient lifeboat at every five miles along their shore, while the Duke of Cornwall, the Heir apparent to England's Crown, cannot boast of one throughout the distance of 150 miles of coast situated at the very portals of the English Channel?"

Fortunately the public conscience was awakened by these revelations and donations to the R.N.L.I. enabled them greatly to extend the lifeboat coverage, so that by 1870 it was as complete as was possible in those days of sail and oar. From 1918 motor lifeboats began to operate on Cornish coasts and the expensive programme of re-equipping all the stations was proceeding well until set back by the Second World War. Due to this the removal of the last sailing and pulling lifeboat was delayed until 1942, but since then a very efficient fleet of motor lifeboats, varying in type and size to suit individual stations and crews, has been available to all in distress, regardless of nationality.

It remains to acknowledge many and varied sources of information. *The Life-boat*, the annual *Reports*, and the *War History* of the Royal National Life-boat Institution have been freely drawn upon. As these accounts are normally brief, the Cornish and national Press has also been referred to, to obtain more detail. Specialised publications, such as the *Mercantile Navy List*, *Lloyd's Register of Shipping*, *Lloyd's*

List and the like, have been used to check names, rigs, and other details of vessels mentioned. The principal local publications on this second section of the Cornish coast are:

Noall, Cyril. *The Story of St. Ives Lifeboat* (1956)

Howarth, Patrick. *The Lifeboat Story* (Chap. x) (1957)

Corin, John. *The Sennen Cove Branch of the R.N.L.I.* (1953)

Williams, Colonel H. W., *Some Reminiscences, 1838-1918* (1918)

Dorrien Smith, Miss Charlotte. *Shipwrecks on the Isles of Scilly* (1950)

du Boulay, Miss Juliet. *Wrecks of the Isles of Scilly* (Reprinted from *The Mariner's Mirror*, 1960)

Grateful acknowledgment is made of the help given by the following individuals and Institutions—Messrs. G. E. Mills, Redruth; C. J. Davies, Truro; Richard Gillis, Newquay; H. L. Douch, Curator of the County Museum, Truro; P. L. Hull, Cornwall County Archivist; R. A. J. Potts, Assistant Archivist; Patrick Howarth, and other officials of the R.N.L.I.; D. C. Vosper, Saltash; John Corin, Penzance and Bristol; Deryk Chappell, Bodmin; Captain Thomas Stevens, Hon. Secretary, R.N.L.I., St. Ives; Stanley Cock, St. Ives; Mrs. M. Harvey, Librarian, Morrab Library, Penzance; Claude Berry, Editor, *West Briton*, Truro; Captain W. Nicholls, Nancegollan; A. W. B. Prowse, Lanteglos-by-Fowey; C. J. Langman, Librarian, Redruth Public Library.

CYRIL NOALL
St. Ives

GRAHAME FARR
Bristol

January 1965

A MAP SHOWING THE PRESENT (underlined) AND PAST LIFEBOAT STATIONS OF CORNWALL

Also St. Mary's and St. Agnes (Isles of Scilly), not shown

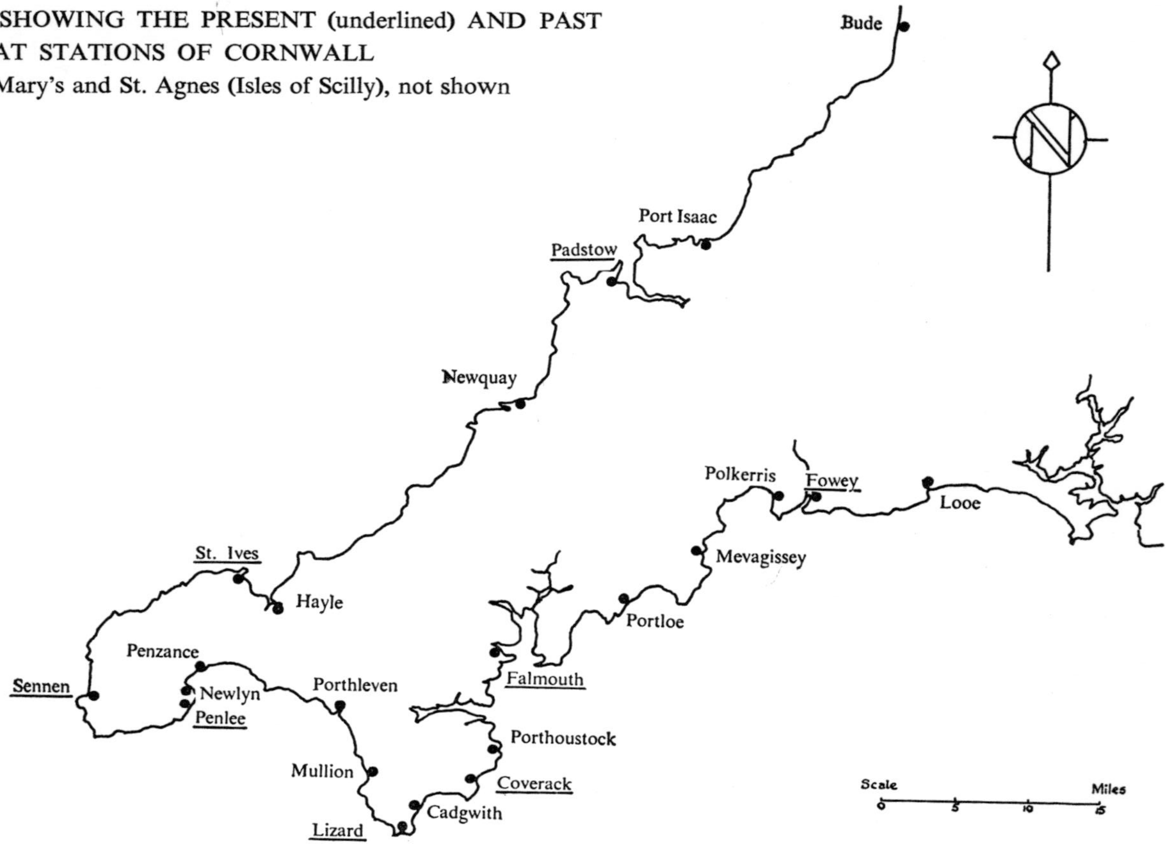

1

ST. IVES

IN THE autumn of 1808, the Rev. Warner, of Bath, undertook a journey through Cornwall, during the course of which he made a special detour to see the ancient fishing port of St. Ives. Describing this place in a book published the following year, he says:

"A strong gale blew" [from the northward] "when we visited it, and threw a terrible sea into the harbour. In general, we were informed, this noble basin was considered as a very safe anchorage, though storms have occurred which covered its surface with wrecks. On the 14th day of the preceding November" [1807] "a melancholy scene of this kind had been exhibited to the inhabitants of St. Ives, when three vessels were thrown upon the rocks of the harbour before their eyes, totally destroyed, and the greater part of their crews swallowed up.

"The affecting sight made its proper impression on some of the spectators, who immediately endeavoured to raise a subscription for building and maintaining a *life-boat*, to prevent in future the most dreadful consequences of such shipwrecks, the loss of the unhappy seamen; but so insensible were the merchants of the place to the dangers and sufferings of the hardy race who fill their coffers, that the philanthropic attempt was frustrated by the impossibility of raising the poor pittance required for the purpose! As we had this information from a merchant of St. Ives, I take it for granted that it is correct. Should it not be so, I must crave pardon of its affluent inhabitants for a representation so disgraceful to their feelings."[1]

The three wrecks were those of the *Atalanta*, lost during the morning under Porthminster Cliff, master and three men drowned; the schooner *Hazard*, from Bristol, thrown ashore near the same place, the master and all the crew, save a little boy, drowned; and the brig *Eliza*, of Exmouth, which stranded in Porthminster Cove, crew saved.

Although more than thirty years were to elapse after Warner's visit before a properly constituted lifeboat station came into being at St. Ives, there is reason to think that even at that early period the town was not entirely lacking in provision for saving life at sea. An old

1. Rev. J. Warner, *A Tour Through Cornwall in the Autumn of 1808.*

retired master mariner informed Mr. Stanley Cock that his grandfather told him as a lad of a little craft shaped like a small seine-boat which used to be kept here for this purpose around the late 1700's. Cork lined, and very lightly constructed, she rowed six oars, the coxswain using a steering oar. Her crew consisted of Royal Navy coastguards, and she was housed in a cellar near the top of "Dick's Hill" (Fish Street).

In the event of a call for assistance, nine men on each side would carry the little boat along to the sea, her crew then clambering on board.

By the middle of the last century the coastguards had adopted naval whalers, which were familiarly known as 'galleys'. They were usually fitted for six or eight rowers, with a further oar used by the Coxswain for steering. Messrs. Lamb and White, of Cowes, patented a lifeboat in similar form about 1843, and large numbers were supplied to the Navy, both for warships and the coastguard. However the boats did not find favour for shore use because of their very limited internal capacity. Nevertheless, coastguards performed many brave rescues in their galleys when nothing else was available. For launching, the one at St. Ives would be taken directly to Porthmeor through a gap in the wall which runs along the eastern half of the beach, when the wind was southerly. Examination of the wall has revealed clear evidence (by St. Christopher's) of such an opening, now built up. With a northerly wind, the launching would be in the harbour by means of the little granite slipway, part of which still remains, on the western side of the Shamrock Lodge.

Much good lifesaving work was undoubtedly performed in St. Ives in those early days, both by the coastguards, and the "hobblers" (pilots), sailors and fishermen.

A classic example of the heroism of these unorganised volunteers was the schooner *Rival*, which grounded at the back of Smeaton's Pier during a heavy gale from the N.W. on the afternoon of December 24th 1838. The local pilots first attempted to rescue the crew by putting off in three six-oared gigs, but failed; and recourse was then had to Manby's apparatus, which also proved ineffectual, owing to the distance to be covered.

Undeterred by these reverses, two seine boats tried to board her, but after encountering several very heavy seas, were carried away to leeward on to Porthminster Beach. The gig *Rasper* was then manned, and succeeded, after various attempts and at great hazard, in getting within a few yards of the vessel. Before a rope could be handed them, their boat was struck and nearly filled by a tremendous sea, and becoming unmanageable, drove on shore and capsized near Pednolver Rocks, the crew narrowly escaping with their lives.

Mr. S. F. Cocking then suggested that one of his pilchard tow-boats should be launched, and this got near enough to the *Rival* to lay hold of a rope. Before they could make it fast, however, a heavy sea forced their boat to leeward. When again attempting to reach the vessel, another tremendous sea broke on board, washing two men overboard, who were, however, miraculously saved by their comrades. The boat, minus several oars, and nearly full of water, finally drove ashore and upset on the beach.

It was now four o'clock, with night fast approaching, whilst the gale continued to rage with unabated fury, promising a watery grave for the *Rival*'s crew. Another crew having volunteered their services, the tow-boat was again launched, and got near the vessel, but was then driven back by the violence of the surf. The pilots, notwithstanding, resumed their oars, and at length succeeded in getting off the crew of five, and landing them on Porthminster Beach. Not content with this, the pilots later managed to get the schooner off and brought her into the pier.

The Shipwreck Society awarded five Silver Medals to those who had played a leading part in this most meritorious service, all being described as either "captains" or "master mariners" in the accompanying citation.

In the same year which witnessed the rescue of the *Rival*'s crew, the Royal Cornwall Polytechnic Society conducted a competition for the best-designed model lifeboat sent for their inspection. Strangely enough, the first two awards were won by entries from St. Ives, the premium offered by Mr. Charles Fox going to Mr. Francis Jennings Adams (1769-1845), a well-known local shipbuilder, and the second prize of two guineas to Mr. John Phillips, schoolmaster.

In preparing his design, Adams sought to achieve two objects; first, to give his vessel the maximum degree of manoeuvrability when near a wreck; and second, to ensure that she should be unsinkable under all circumstances. The first of these aims he achieved by fitting his model with two bows, so that, both ends being alike, she was always in a position either to go ahead or astern. The rowers effected this change of direction by turning round and sitting on opposite sides of the same thwarts and pulling from a different set of thowels. This change round could be performed in much less than a minute, without the risk of winding or backing. Provision was made for six rowers, with a steersman at either end, each of whom also had an oar, to be used in place of a rudder. The lifeboat's buoyancy was assured by the fitting of an air-tight vessel of from 30 to 50 gallons capacity under the decks at each end. This could be made of either tin-plate, copper, or india-rubber cloth; or, as an alternative, a quantity of good cork might be employed.

The Adams lifeboat was clinker-built, and fitted up like a gig, with bottom boards and stretchers, and with the upper strake lined inside and out with cork to add to its buoyancy. It was estimated that the boat would not sink even when full of water and with twenty men on board, and that if capsized, she would immediately right herself again. The lifeboat was to have the following dimensions: extreme length, 30 ft.; breadth, 5 ft. 8 in. moulded; extreme breadth amidships, 5 ft. 10in.; depth midships, 2 ft. 2 in. The mean breadth line was calculated as the segment of a circle from one end to the other, having a radius of 41 ft. 6 in., the water lines being parts of circles of greater radii.[1]

The favourable reception accorded to Mr. Adams' design led to a proposal being made for a lifeboat, constructed in accordance with his proposals, to be built and stationed at St. Ives. Adams himself was asked to build the lifeboat; and her first launching took place on January 11th 1840. A description of the ceremony reads: "Manned by nine St. Ives pilots, under the command of Mr. Martin, chief officer of the coastguard, she was rowed by eight oars, and steered with an oar over each end. Although she is considerably larger and heavier than six-oared pilot gigs, she outstripped one and kept equal pace with two others brought out to be rowed against her. In a rough sea, she is expected to have great advantage over them. She floated buoyantly when filled with water, having her own crew and eight or ten other men on board, and would have borne up as many more as could have found place in her, at least 15 or 20, the weight of the whole crew standing upon the gunwhale having been insufficient to effect it. The boat has been found to answer exceedingly well, and there is no doubt that, in the hands of our bold and skilful seamen, she will be the means, under Providence, of saving many valuable lives from destruction."

The first service of this new lifeboat—appropriately named the *Hope*—took place only a few months later, on April 7th 1840. During a heavy northerly gale, the smack *Mary Ann*, of Poole, laden with culm from Swansea, drove on shore near Pednolver Point, the mast soon

1. Rep. R.C.P.S., 1838, p. 143.

after going by the board. In two attempts to reach the vessel the lifeboat was thrown back upon the beach by the violence of the sea and filled with water. Two men then swam off to the smack, and at the imminent risk of their own lives, succeeded in saving the crew.

This represents the only known service record of this lifeboat. She was, however, still stationed here in 1852; for on May 27th of that year, Mr. H. T. Richardson, of Bala, arrived at St. Ives to demonstrate a new tubular lifeboat he had invented, which he offered to row against the local boat. The *Hope*'s crew, however, refused the challenge.

The Northumberland Report (1851) states that in 1848 the Adams lifeboat was kept under a shed 400 yards from high-water mark in charge of a "Mr. Hockin"[1]. The date of its building is wrongly given as 1836. "With slight repairs, and proper internal fittings," this report continues, "she might be made a useful boat." There was no boat-house or carriage, but the station possessed one 24 lb. mortar.

The late Mr. Thomas Warren (who died a centenarian) remembered the old lifeboat, when out of use, lying near the Ropewalk, her cork lining slowly rotting away. A St. Ives fisherman who had lost his boat through getting an overload of herrings, bought the old craft, which he reconditioned and used for fishing locally.

Mr. Kent Leddra, of St. Ives, still possesses the original model of the *Hope* made in 1838 by his relative, Mr. Adams. This is in an excellent state of preservation, having been recently restored; and with its smooth, flowing lines, affords striking proof of Mr. Adams' skill as a designer of small boats. The late Mr. R. M. Nance (a well-known authority on maritime history) has stated that "the influence of the design of the Adams lifeboat contributed greatly to the design of the fishing gigs built for many years in St. Ives afterwards; their gigs were fifty years in advancement of similar craft built in the Mount's Bay area."[2]

A very gallant rescue, which attracted the favourable notice of the Lifeboat Institution, was performed at St. Ives on December 20th 1854 by volunteer crews using local seine and pilot boats. The schooner *Swift*, of Exeter, bound from Newport to Sheerness with iron, and having a crew of six on board, grounded on the sandbank off Pednolver Point whilst running for St. Ives Pier during a northerly gale. Very soon afterwards her fate was shared by the schooner *Concord*, of Looe,

1. Possibly Samuel *Hocking* (Mayor in 1854) a gentleman who greatly interested himself in local shipping and harbour matters.

2. MS. note by R. M. Nance, at St. Ives Museum.

from Neath to Southampton with coal, also with a crew of six. This vessel struck on the same bank, but further out from shore.

The tide was then half-ebb; had it been flood, all the men on both schooners would probably have been lost. Even as it was, their situation appeared perilous in the extreme. They could do nothing to help themselves, and clung on desperately for survival as the waves broke over their vessels—those of the *Swift* to the bowsprit and those of the *Concord* to the rigging. Moved to action by their pitiable plight, some local men launched a large seine boat belonging to Messrs. Bolitho, Hichens and Co., in which a strenuous but unsuccessful effort was made to reach the wrecks. One of the light pilot-gigs—perhaps of all boats the safest and most manageable in a heavy gale—was thereupon launched, and reached the *Swift*, whose crew she took off and landed. The gig, however, proved unavailing in the breakers around the *Concord*, and so the seine-boat was again brought into service, accompanied this time by another boat belonging to the Cornwall Company, together with two gigs to assist should the large boats be swamped.

After a desperate struggle through the broken water, the boats succeeded in reaching the *Concord*'s bowsprit. The sailors who were then in the fore-rigging slid down the forestay and were all saved. The master, however, had unfortunately taken refuge in the main-rigging, and in attempting to get forward was thrown into the sea and lost. The manner in which these rescues were carried out under very difficult and dangerous circumstances reflected great credit on all concerned. A public subscription for the four boats' crews realised £152 18s., the Lifeboat Institution contributing £10. The two wrecks which remained firmly embedded in the sand, constituted a great danger to the seining industry. After a diver had removed about 40 tons of iron from the *Swift*, the seine owners purchased both schooners, and on August 31st 1855, raised the *Swift* with the help of two light vessels.

On March 10th 1860, a public meeting was convened at the Town Hall to "consider the necessity of forming a lifeboat station at St. Ives" under the auspices of the R.N.L.I. Success attended this effort, a local branch of the Institution being formed, and a boathouse was built near the Island on a site presented by the Earl of Mornington. Its cost of £142 was partly defrayed by Mr. T. J. A. Robartes, M.P., a gentleman who rendered great service to the lifeboat cause in Cornwall at this period.

These preparations being completed, the R.N.L.I. forwarded one of its lifeboats to St. Ives in July 1861. Called the *Moses*, this boat, which cost £154 to build, was the anonymous gift of a lady who had, in the previous year, presented the first lifeboat, named *Joshua*, to the Newquay station. The *Moses* came from Messrs. Forrestt, of Limehouse, being of the self-righting type, clinker-built, length 30 ft., beam 7 ft., displacement 30 cwt., and rowing six oars, single-banked.

When the lifeboat, with her carriage, was being taken to the new boathouse, it was found that one of the streets—"Dick's Hill", or Fish Street—leading from the Wharf to the Island was too narrow for the carriage to pass, so that she had to be temporarily secured on the sand near the Custom House. Her first launch took place in mid-September when she was rowed round the Head to Porthmeor Beach and brought into the broken surf. Here the boat was kept for some time, with the seas breaking all round and over her. After returning to the pier, the crew, part of whom belonged to the coastguard, donned their lifebelts, jumped overboard, and remained swimming about for some time, watched by hundreds of spectators on the hills and beach.

From her boathouse (which still stands, now a store, opposite the old Island Road school) the *Moses* could be removed to any part of the coast with the greatest of ease. According to an old St. Ives resident,[1] this lifeboat was always launched from the northern side of the harbour; but tradition speaks of her being launched also from Porthgwidden and Porthmeor beaches. On one occasion, however, during a practice at Porthmeor, the lifeboat was picked up by a heavy sea, and thrown on the beach, where she had to remain lying under the cliff for an entire week-end. After this mishap, she was never launched there again[2].

Her first service took place on June 12th 1863, when the schooners *Superior* and *Emma*, both of St. Ives, and *Azores Packet*, of Falmouth, all went ashore just outside the harbour whilst running in for shelter during a heavy gale. The crews of all three vessels were saved, those on board the *Azores Packet*, which had grounded on a sandbank at the

1. Evidence given by Capt. Care before a Local Government Board enquiry at St. Ives regarding the Chy-an-Chy slipway, mentioned in *St. Ives Times*, January 6th 1922.

2. Information per Mr. Stanley Cock, St. Ives. A lively description of a Porthmeor practice launch is also given in the *Royal Cornwall Gazette* January 2nd 1863. The wind blew strong from N.W. with a very heavy surf on the beach; "so great, indeed, were the mountain surges that there was a difficulty to get men to man her from among the dauntless and heroic St. Ives men. At length she went off with two hands short, there being but seven on board. After two or three ineffectual efforts to scale the towering breakers, away she dashed amidst the cheers of hundreds who had stood expecting to see her thrown helpless on the shore."

harbour entrance, being taken off with great difficulty. After this, Coxswain Levett and his men took warps on board the schooner to try to save the vessel, but failed, the *Azores Packet* having filled with water. "The service rendered by the lifeboat", says a contemporary account, "was prompt and noble, there being a tremendous sea running. The *Moses* at one time was completely under water and lost three oars."

The most famous service of this little lifeboat took place on October 28th 1865, when the French brig *Providence*, of Granville, was wrecked on the western spit of Hayle Bar during a severe gale. The lifeboat left the pier to go to her assistance just before 8 a.m. On crossing Hayle Bar, she broke her drogue-rope in a very heavy sea, and flew before the storm in an almost perpendicular position, her bow completely submerged. She then overturned, throwing out all hands except the Coxswain and Second Coxswain, who both were under the boat until she righted—a period of at least two minutes. The remainder of the crew regained the boat, except one man who had been driven some distance away; but he was presently picked up. Undaunted they succeeded in getting the boat into the channel to leeward of the ship, but owing to the strong undertow the lifeboat could not be placed alongside. After persevering for at least half an hour, they managed to approach within a hundred yards, and brought the boat up, being unable to venture nearer. The crew of the French vessel then prepared a raft, on which three men were able to float close to the bow of the *Moses*. Unfortunately, three or four heavy seas broke over them, and swept two away to their deaths, the third sailor reaching the lifeboat only with great difficulty. He was scarcely taken on board when the *Moses* again capsized, but righted in less than a minute. The Captain of the *Providence* and two seamen then put off from the wreck in their small boat, but this was soon swamped in the raging seas. The lifeboatmen, pulling valiantly to their assistance, succeeded in picking them up, and brought all the rescued men safely to harbour. For this courageous and heroic piece of work, the R.N.L.I. voted a Silver Medal to Coxswain Levett, and monetary awards to him and his crew. In addition to this, £115 was raised by public subscription and divided among them. But the most notable award of all came from Napoleon III, Emperor of the French, who sent a Gold Medal for the Coxswain and a Silver Medal for each member of the crew, the first awards of their kind ever gained by a British lifeboat crew.

Another memorable service of the *Moses* took place on January 11th

1866, when the s.s. *Bessie*, of Hayle, was beached on Lelant sands during a terrible storm. The little lifeboat, after making three heroic but unsuccessful efforts to reach the steamer through the terrible seas and strong set of the tide, joined forces with the ten-oared *Richard Lewis* from Penzance, the first lifeboat rescuing three, and the second the remaining six of the *Bessie*'s crew. Because of the weather, both

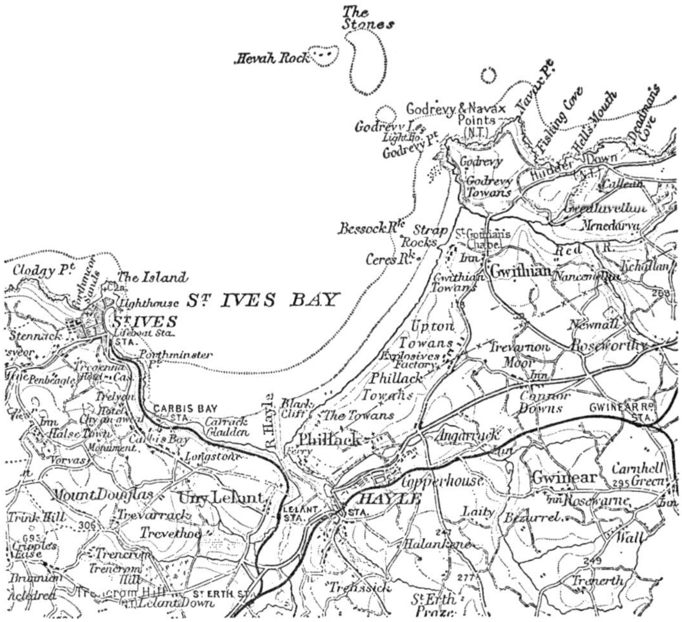

lifeboats were taken overland to the scene of the wreck, the *Richard Lewis* being hauled on her carriage by eight horses.

This was the last service of the old *Moses*. Although she had acquitted herself nobly, a larger and more powerful boat was needed and a new and more suitable lifeboat was built for the station. She arrived here in June 1866, being forwarded free of charge by the G.W.R. and associated companies. This boat bore the same name as her predecessor, rowed ten oars, double-banked, and was presented by the same anonymous donor.

The new lifeboat proved too large for the old boat-house, whilst difficulties also arose in getting her into the harbour, in consequence of the then very narrow entrance to Fish Street. Accordingly, in 1867, the Committee acquired premises at Market Strand, known as the Old Custom House, on which the present lifeboat house was erected by Mr. Sampson Noall at a cost of £140. From here, the boat was launched straight over the Fore Sand, which at that time rose level to the boathouse door.

The new *Moses* quickly proved her worth at such wrecks as those of the *Mary Lewis*, the *Gypsy*, and the *Queen*; but inevitably there were occasions when, despite the efforts of her crew, complete success was not achieved. One such tragedy took place on December 2nd 1867, when the French brig *Courrier du Nord*, of Morlaix (190 tons) from Swansea to Algiers with 252 tons of coal, went ashore at St. Ives after being crippled in heavy weather near the Longships. She had eight men on board—the Captain, mate and six hands. A strong gale was blowing from the N.E. when she struck, with bow to wind and waves, on the Ridge. On this the seas were breaking with such fearful violence that only a few hours previously they had broken down the end of the newly-built Wood Pier, which then formed a large outer harbour on the seaward side of Smeaton's Pier. The brig stranded but a cable's length from the shattered circular end of this Wood Pier, but none of the St. Ives pilot boats dared venture out to her.

However, the *Moses* had been brought out in readiness before the brig struck, and so was in a position immediately to make her way to the vessel. The tremendous sea and strong current beat her to leeward of the *Courrier du Nord*, and she only brought up to windward of the wreck with much difficulty. A grapnel line was thrown aboard the brig, but despite every care in working the boat, and with the bowman hauling on the line, the rowers could hardly hold their own. At length the grapnel hooks straightened out under the tremendous strain, and the *Moses* was then driven far to leeward, and when rowing up along the shore to regain a windward berth, a man who had jumped overboard from the wreck was seen floating on a lifebuoy in the water outside. The boat made towards him and managed to pull him up in a greatly exhausted condition. She then rowed to the pier to land him and take on a fresh crew.

A second rescue attempt was made by veering down on the ship by a warp from the New Pier. When the lifeboat got to the brig, a grapnel was again successfully thrown, and the crew were asked to make the line secure, but they seemed either benumbed or panic-stricken, and never stirred. The grapnel eventually came away and the *Moses* once more returned to the pier and took aboard a third crew.

The next attempt was made without a warp, and in going round to windward of the brig, a heavy sea struck the lifeboat, washing one of the crew out of her. In picking him up, two larboard oars were lost, and for want of them the boat was driven ashore on Porthminster beach. Before she could be launched again, the brig herself drifted on the rising tide to Porthminster, where her mainmast went by the board, carrying with it most of the crew, who had taken refuge in the main rigging. Two others left the wreck in the ship's boat, which had parted from the stern davits; one of these was drowned when the boat capsized soon after they had got into her, but the other hung on till she drifted to Carrack Rock, at the south-eastern end of Porthminster beach. Here he was dashed out and carried towards Porthminster Rock, followed on shore by hundreds of spectators. A number of these made unsuccessful efforts to save the drowning man, at great personal risk; and eventually the sailor, now motionless, was seized by a young St. Ives man, who, assisted by others, some of whom were much injured by being dashed against the rocks by the breakers, hauled him on shore, apparently dead, but he eventually recovered.

Two men only could now be seen on the brig; one of these was killed by a heavy sea, whilst the survivor came away on the stern rail, but was drowned before the lifeboat could put off to his assistance. The *Moses*, with a fourth crew, made a final, unavailing effort to reach the brig, in case anyone remained alive on her, but the vessel was, in fact, deserted. Despite the heroic efforts which had been made by her crews, some criticism was afterwards expressed of the way in which the *Moses* had been handled, although a subsequent enquiry fully vindicated the conduct of the lifeboatmen on this melancholy occasion.

Better fortune attended them on February 2nd 1873 when they rescued the crews of three vessels wrecked at St. Ives in a severe storm. During the morning, the schooners *Mary Ann* and *Rambler*, of Plymouth, and the brig *Frances*, of Porthcawl, which had anchored in the Bay the previous night, were all driven ashore near the harbour. It was dead low water, and the lifeboat (by then re-named *Covent Garden*) could only be launched with the greatest difficulty. The *Rambler* had run aground near the New Pier and two men in the rigging were washed overboard. One disappeared after a while, but the other, the Captain, supported by a piece of timber, was picked up by the lifeboat. Of the two men who still remained on board, one was washed overboard and drowned, but the other was taken off by the *Covent Garden*.

The lifeboat, with a fresh crew, next dropped down on the *Mary Ann*, which had grounded under Pednolver Point, and saved the five half-frozen members of her crew. Having landed these, the lifeboat then put off with a third crew to rescue those on the *Frances*. She was, however, swept by the current almost to Porthminster Point and driven on the beach.

Hundreds of men and women hauled the *Covent Garden* in, clear of the breakers, put ropes on her and dragged the boat across the beach to windward of the brig. With a fresh crew of volunteers, Coxswain Murphy went afloat for the fifth time and after a gallant struggle reached the *Frances* and rescued her crew of six. Two, who never left the boat during the five attempts, each received the Silver Medal of the Institution.

For many years James Murphy served as Second Coxswain of the St. Ives lifeboat under Paul Curnow, whom he later succeeded as Coxswain. These two men were responsible for effecting many gallant rescues, typical of these being the service they performed to the French schooner *Rosa Josephs* on January 18th 1881. Early that morning, the vessel was seen at anchor off Porthminster Point, there being then a storm from E.N.E. with tremendous seas and a heavy snowfall. Realising she must soon drive ashore, the lifeboat (again re-named *Exeter*) was launched at eight o'clock, with Coxswain Curnow in charge. She got afloat only with the greatest difficulty, one heavy sea knocking several oars out of the men's hands. Getting outside, however, the combined force of the wind and waves drove the *Exeter* back into the harbour. A second attempt to reach the distressed vessel was made at ten o'clock, and the lifeboat again pulled towards her in the teeth of the gale to rescue her crew of five, not a moment too soon, as the vessel parted when the lifeboat was close to her and shortly after went to pieces on the rocks at Porthminster Point. The *Rosa Josephs* (87 tons), of St. Vaast, was bound from Briton Ferry to Cherbourg, with coal. Four oars were broken aboard the lifeboat on this service, and she also sustained minor damage to her rudder.

The *Exeter* performed another fine piece of work the following year when she launched to the aid of the St. Ives fishing luggers *Quick* and *Gyles* during the great "April Gale" on April 2nd 1882. On that day, the wind, which was about N.W., blew from about 11 a.m. till 3 in the afternoon with tremendous fury, lashing the sea into foam, and causing the spray to form a fog so dense that nothing could be distinguished beyond a quarter of a mile from shore. A large part of the St. Ives fleet of over a hundred mackerel boats was out, and much anxiety was felt for their safety. The s.s. *Drumhendry* broke from her moorings in the Bay, and went ashore at Gwithian, her crew being rescued by the Hayle lifeboat, whilst a schooner, the *Ellen Vair*, rode out the storm, but seemed in such imminent danger that the *Exeter* was taken down to the water's edge in readiness.

Some of the missing luggers fetched home as the day wore on, but two others came in late at nearly low water, and had to anchor beyond the Ridge, on which the sea was breaking with such fury that none of the gigs could venture outside to take off their exhausted crews. The lifeboat was therefore launched a second time, and took off fresh crews to relieve those on board the fishing boats, bringing the men ashore in such an exhausted state that they had to be assisted to their homes. But for this timely relief, many of these fourteen fishermen would probably have died from exposure. The station records show that three horses were used to assist in launching the lifeboat on this occasion—a practice often followed at St. Ives in the old days for low-water launches.

In September 1886 a new lifeboat arrived at St. Ives, two feet longer than her predecessor, measuring 34 ft. by 7½ ft., and rowing ten oars. Provided by the legacy of William Kendall, Esq., of Exeter, she took the name of this city, which had also been borne by the previous boat since 1878. Her first service took place on March 21st 1889, when she saved four from the ketch *Wave*, of Gloucester (83 tons), in ballast from Padstow to Lydney, which stranded within the harbour during a strong N.N.E. gale.

Between 1888 and 1890 several important alterations were carried out in St. Ives harbour, including the building of the Victoria Extension to Smeaton's Pier and the piercing of three arches in the latter structure to sluice sand from the harbour. As a result of these changes, the beach level before the boathouse door dropped considerably. To meet the launching difficulty thereby created, Messrs. Lang and Son (contractors for the above works) during the summer of 1890 laid down the first lifeboat slipway ever built at St. Ives. This extended at right-angles from the boathouse door. Part of it is still visible, the remainder now being covered by the Wharf Road (built in 1922). In 1891 a powerful winch was fixed in the boathouse to facilitate the launching and hauling up of the lifeboat over the slip. In February 1894, owing to the erection of the West Pier, the floor of the boathouse and the eastern half of its walls and roof had to be raised several feet, a new loft constructed, the doorway heightened, and higher doors fixed.

Coxswain Paul Curnow retired in March 1889, being succeeded in that post by James Murphy. Mr. Curnow received the Institution's Second Service Clasp, a certificate of service, and £20 for "his long and valuable services as Coxswain of the lifeboat on this station, and . . . the courage, steadiness and intrepidity that he had displayed during the 26½ years of his service."

In March 1893 the *Exeter* was sent to London to be fitted with a drop keel and other improvements then being introduced in self-righting lifeboats. Her place was filled by the lifeboat *Reserve No. 7*, which remained till October 1894. During this period, on November 18th 1893, St. Ives was visited by the terrible "Cintra Gale". Three steamers—the *Vulture* (281 tons), *Cintra* (291 tons) and *Bessie* (153 tons)[1]—all coal laden, were driven ashore on Carbis Bay beach, where they had been trying to ride out the storm. The *Reserve No. 7* was immediately manned but could not leave the harbour owing to the tremendous sea on the Ridge. Landward egress from the town was also blocked by construction work then in progress on the new West Pier. However, the rocket apparatus crew succeeded in rescuing twelve from the *Vulture* and eight from the *Bessie* (their entire crews) with five more from the *Cintra*, although seven of those on the last vessel were drowned. *Vulture* and *Cintra* soon after became total wrecks, the *Bessie* also being almost entirely under water. A fearful gale from N.N.W. raged with tremendous seas whilst these rescues were being effected, the Bay being one mass of foam as far as the eye could see.

This happened during the morning. In the afternoon, the s.s. *Rosedale* (590 tons), of London, in ballast, was run on shore at Porthminster Beach. The lifeboat was again launched, and at great risk crossed the Ridge but failed to reach the steamer. A succession of heavy seas drove the boat ashore broadside on Porthminster Beach close to the *Rosedale* with five oars broken off short and two of the deck air cases holed. It was found impossible to launch the lifeboat again, and the steamer's crew of sixteen were rescued by the rocket apparatus. This was Murphy's last launch, and though unsuccessful, perhaps the most gallant of them all, for he was a dying man when he put off to the *Rosedale* in that terrible storm.

James Murphy was succeeded as Coxswain by Thomas Quick in 1895, and under his command the lifeboat carried out many valuable services to local fishing boats and coasting vessels. Two noteworthy, though unsuccessful, launches were performed by him on September

1. The same vessel which had stranded at Lelant in 1866.

25th 1896, when the full-rigged ship *Alexander Yeats*, of Liverpool. (1500 tons), with pitch-pine from Darien (Ga.) to Devonport was sighted in distress with her sails blown away somewhere near Portreath, during a whole N.W. gale. On neither occasion did the lifeboat make contact and the ship was eventually wrecked at Gurnard's Head, her crew being saved by rocket apparatus. The Hayle lifeboat, assisted by the steam tug *North Star*, also made an ineffectual attempt to reach the *Alexander Yeats* as she drifted westwards across the Bay, but dared not venture over the Bar because of the heavy seas. On January 1st 1900, a new and larger lifeboat for the St. Ives station, named the *James Stevens No. 10*, arrived at Hayle, and the next day was brought by water to St. Ives. The *Exeter*, meanwhile, was placed on the Quay under coverings pending her removal to Poplar on March 21st 1901. She actually performed one further service before her retirement, when the ketch *Star*, of Scilly (50 tons), with coal from Cardiff to Scilly, missed stays in attempting to enter the harbour during a heavy N.N.W. gale on November 7th 1900. She anchored, and showed signals of distress. The *Exeter* launched at 7.30 a.m. and took off the crew of three shortly before the ketch dragged her anchors and drifted on the rocks at Porthminster Point where she became a total wreck.

The *James Stevens No. 10* made her first service launch on November 6th 1900, when the local fishing gig *Fortitude*, which had been caught in a N.N.W. storm, was driven on the Western Spits with the loss of three lives. Though unable to render any assistance to the gig, the lifeboat stood by five luggers, which had been fishing in Basset's Bay, whilst they waited for the flood tide to cross the Ridge into the harbour. During the next 33 years the *James Stevens* achieved a magnificent record of service at St. Ives, saving a total of 227 lives—more than that recorded by many a whole station in the county. It is unfortunately impossible to do more than describe a few highlights of the career of this wonderful old lifeboat.

On February 5th 1901, the brigantine *Julien Marie*, of Auray (73 tons), with coal from Swansea to Bordeaux, was observed running for St. Ives harbour during a heavy N.N.E. gale. After the vessel had burned flares, the *James Stevens* put off and made for her. The brigantine, carrying only mainstaysail and lower topsail, hauled to, and tried to enter the harbour; but the heavy sea, together with the "drag" caused by her broken foretopmast with yards, sails, and jibboom trailing in the water, made this impossible, and she began drifting fast to leeward. She dropped an anchor, which did not hold; and seeing their vessel was doomed, the crew of six, together with a dog, came off in the lifeboat. The *Julien Marie* soon after went ashore on Porthminster Beach and became a total wreck.

On October 16th 1907, the schooner *Susan Elizabeth*, of St. Ives (130 tons), left the Mumbles for her home port with a cargo of coal. A heavy N.N.E. gale then sprang up, which rapidly increased in strength, and fears were apprehended for the vessel's safety. In expectation of her arrival, the lifeboat was launched in readiness, and throughout the night in a bitter gale and drenching rain the crew stuck at their post, ready to start at any moment.

Early on the morning of the 17th, with the tide ebbing and the *Susan Elizabeth* not yet in sight, she was beached and put on her carriage in the harbour. Soon after six o'clock, however, the schooner appeared off the Head under lower topsail and standing jib, running for the pier. The *James Stevens* was again launched, and reached the vessel just after she struck on the Ridge, but a strong tide at once carried the boat to leeward. Five times she was rowed towards the vessel, each time getting close, but as often was swept away, and eventually cast ashore on Porthminster Beach. The vessel's crew were seen huddled together in the bow while the seas made a clean breach over her. Scores of fishermen and others tried to refloat the lifeboat, and after three quarters of an hour's strenuous efforts succeeded in getting her off.

Hard pulling by the crew brought her again alongside the *Susan Elizabeth* and they then rescued her crew of four, who were safely landed in the harbour. Shortly after, the vessel broke in two, and by 11.30 a.m. there was nothing to be seen of her but the masts, and a few spars and ropes floating in the water. Serving in the lifeboat's crew on this occasion was Mr. John Curnow, son of the *Susan*'s master, who also had another son with him on the schooner.

On January 7th 1908, at about 9.15 p.m., the three-masted schooner *Lizzie R. Wilce* (252 tons), of Falmouth, with anthracite from Swansea to St. Malo and a crew of five, was seen running for the harbour, in a heavy N.W. gale. On nearing the entrance, however, she missed stays, and after first striking on Pednolver Rocks, was driven on to Porthminster Beach. The *James Stevens* was launched at 9.30 and rowed to the distressed vessel, and after some difficulty succeeded in rescuing her crew, returning to harbour in the teeth of the gale.

At 4.40 a.m. the next morning, with the gale still raging, the lifeboat, which had been housed only two and a half hours previously, was again launched to go to the assistance of another three-masted schooner, the *Mary Barrow*, of Barrow (250 tons), bound with anthracite from Swansea to Medina Mills, I.o.W. This vessel, in running for the harbour, struck heavily on the Ridge, and then started to beat ashore towards Porthminster. The lifeboat got to windward of her, dropped anchor, and veered down; and after a great deal of risk rescued the crew of five. The spectacle presented at daybreak by these two fine sailing ships ashore together on the same beach was a striking one, and has fortunately been preserved by the camera. The *Lizzie R. Wilce* became a total wreck, but the *Mary Barrow* was eventually refloated.

The St. Ives station produced a fine service record during the First World War. Two Silver Medals were awarded, one to Coxswain Thomas Stevens for saving nine of the crew of the s.s. *Taunton* (142 tons), off Gwithian, and the other to a Mr. Henry Escott (not a member of the crew) for life-saving when a Government motor launch, previously in difficulties in the Bay, blew up when driven ashore at Clodgy Point.

The service to the *Taunton* was a particularly meritorious one. This steamer, bound from Newport for Rouen with French military stores, was in a dangerous position off Gwithian Beach at about noon on December 27th 1915. She had been forced to seek shelter in the Bay in a strong W.N.W. gale, but her anchors failed to hold and she gradually dragged across to the eastern shore. About 2 p.m. the master hoisted a distress signal; the lifeboat immediately responded, and after a difficult launch sailed down wind to the scene. The steamer was rolling heavily and had a broken rudder post, which made it impossible for her to help herself by the engines. Being on a dead lee shore it would have been folly to go alongside with a pulling boat, so the coxswain anchored and veered down. A rope was floated to the steamer, and by this means an endless whip and lifebuoy were rigged up, the nine men being hauled to safety through the sea. The return journey proved the most difficult part of the rescue, made in the teeth of the terrific sea and a strong flood tide. It took three and a half hours of hard pulling, darkness having fallen before they arrived back in the harbour. Three of the rescued were very exhausted, and one severely injured. Meanwhile the *Taunton's* anchors had at last secured a hold, so the steam tug *Helen Peele* was summoned from Padstow, and on the 28th the steamer was towed into harbour and beached.

One of the most dramatic services performed at this time was that to the s.s. *Kintuck*, mined or torpedoed about six miles N.W. of St. Ives at about 1.30 p.m. on December 2nd 1917. A moderate northerly gale was blowing at the time, accompanied by a rough sea. It being then dead low water, the boat had to be taken over the beach, across the Ridge by means of the pushing poles, and then launched into deep water, getting away at about 2.15 p.m. The *Kintuck* had gone down by the stern, her crew of 54 taking to the boats. This steamer, a vessel of 7,000 tons gross, was then serving as an Admiralty transport, and was bound from London to Barry in ballast.

Making several tacks, the lifeboat reached one of the ship's boats, and after taking the men out of her, went to two other boats which were trying to make for the Head. Their crews also were trans-shipped, and the *James Stevens* then proceeded to a fourth boat. The coxswain, finding she was manned by firemen, placed one of his crew on board to take charge, and accompanied her into the harbour, where they safely landed a total of 34 men.

The Captain and Chief Officer, with eight men, were picked up by a French steamer and taken to Swansea. Yet another of the ship's boats, with nine men on board, ran before the wind, and was driven on shore between the Carracks and Mussel Point, just to the eastward of Wicca Pool. The boat was smashed to pieces on the rocks, and one of the firemen on board drowned.

The sound of the explosion when the *Kintuck* was mined had been plainly heard at Treveal Farm, some little distance inland from Wicca Pool; and the farmer's grandson, aged about sixteen, hastened down to the cliff, where he guided the survivors to safety. The eight men were taken to the farm, supplied with food and dry clothing, and then despatched on the farm wain to St. Ives.

Mr. Stevens resigned as Coxswain at the end of the War, being succeeded by Mr. Robert Wedge, under whose charge the boat effected many gallant services. The first of these occurred on January 2nd 1920, when the s.s. *Valur*, of Reykjavik (350 tons), with coal from Newport to France, sprang a leak off the Longships, her pumps at the same time being choked. She was sighted drifting north off Sennen at ten p.m., but the lifeboat there could not be launched, and so the St. Ives station was notified. The *James Stevens* got afloat just before eleven, and in the teeth of a strong S.S.E. gale and ground swell, proceeded about four miles west of Clodgy Point. Here, lights were observed in the offing, which the lifeboatmen answered, and then headed towards the *Valur*. The Captain, afraid the steamer would keep afloat only a few minutes longer, wished to beach her, but the coxswain persuaded him to try to get the ship into St. Ives. Two lifeboatmen were put aboard the

Valur, which was still able to proceed under her own steam, and taking the boat in tow, they made for St. Ives Head. When off Porthmeor beach, the master altered his course, and was running his ship for the beach, whereupon the lifeboatmen took charge and eventually at about one a.m. got the vessel safely into harbour. None too soon did the *Valur* reach port, for by that time the engine room had been flooded.

One of Coxswain Wedge's most remarkable achievements was the rescue, during one day, of forty men from ten vessels in distress in St. Ives Bay. Just before midnight on July 28th 1921, a sudden gale sprang up from N.N.W., throwing a heavy sea into the Bay, where a fleet of over thirty Breton fishing boats and other vessels ran for safety. Among them was a ketch, the *H. F. Bolt*, of Bideford, bound from Avonmouth to Hayle with a cargo of maize; and at about 5.45 a.m. on the 29th she was seen to be dragging her anchors, and shortly afterwards showed signals for assistance. The lifeboat was quickly launched, and took off the crew of three, and brought them safely to the harbour.

About 8.40 another ketch, the *Anne*, of Gloucester, with maize from Avonmouth to Truro, signalled for assistance; the lifeboat at once responded, and the four hands on board were also brought into the harbour. Shortly after ten the *James Stevens* put off to the assistance of one of the French crabbers, the *St. Eloi*, from which she took off four men and a boy. A fourth call was made from another French fishing vessel the *Suzanne Yvonne*, about 11 o'clock, resulting in another crew of four hands being taken on board and duly landed.

Still the calls for help kept coming from the crabbers—the *St. Mauday*, *Eclair*, *Turquoise*, *Anne Marie*, *En Avant* and *Providence*—and from each, Coxswain Wedge and his men rescued a crew of four hands. A very turbulent sea prevailed all the while, the distressed craft being tossed about by the huge waves and the crew's dexterous handling of their lifeboat received great praise from those who watched the scene from the West Pier and other vantage points.

During 1922 extensive alterations were carried out to St. Ives harbour, which made necessary a change in the manner of launching the lifeboat. Before this time, there had been no roadway connecting the West Pier with the Wharf at Chy-an-Chy, but only (for part of the way) a narrow footpath. Construction of the Wharf Road during that year rendered the old lifeboat slip unusable. Accordingly, the slipway at Chy-an-Chy, originally built for cargo and fish landing purposes, was widened and adapted as a lifeboat slip. For launching, the boat was drawn on its carriage from its boathouse along the Wharf Road to Chy-an-Chy, and thence over the slip into the harbour. This method is still in use today, except that a tractor is now used for hauling and launching.

During the early morning of December 22nd 1922, the s.s. *Eleanor*, of London, from Barry to Portugal with 2,000 tons of coal, was sighted sending up distress signals about eight miles N.W. of St. Ives Head. She had lost her propeller a few hours previously in a gale off Pendeen, and was in a helpless condition. The lifeboat crew were summoned shortly before seven o'clock, but experienced difficulty in getting the *James Stevens* off the slipway owing to the tremendous ground sea. Outside the harbour, the conditions were so bad that the boat could not carry more than double-reef canvas, and they had continually to ease her along the sea.

When the lifeboatmen first sighted the steamer, she was down to windward four miles ahead, the tide being to windward of the ship. They got abreast of her at nine o'clock during a tremendous hail shower —"a white squall", to use the coxswain's description—which made it impossible to do anything aboard the boat except maintain their position. After the squall had passed, they stayed the lifeboat and with the help of their jib ran in under the lee of the steamer. The Captain at first refused to come off, but as the lifeboat was leaving, the ship's crew beckoned her to return, as they wished to be taken ashore. The lifeboat accordingly went back and was hauled up to the steamer with two grappling lines, and the men were told to drop into her whenever a chance presented itself. The *Eleanor* was rising and falling in the trough of the sea, which at times washed right over her. However, they had a little shelter under her lee, and some of the men dropped into the boat itself, others being caught by the lifeboatmen. When it was thought everyone else had come off, the Captain himself left, this operation taking about half an hour; but no sooner had they pushed off than three more men came out of the forecastle, some of whom had apparently been asleep below. To get them off, the grappling line had to be thrown three times before the boat could again be hitched up to the ship. Eventually, however, all sixteen hands were safely taken aboard, and the lifeboat shoved off, reaching her station about eleven o'clock. Meanwhile, the *Eleanor* continued to drift, and about two in the afternoon struck the Stones, near Godrevy lighthouse. Terrific seas were breaking clean over Godrevy and the island rock, and within half-an-hour these had pounded the 1,200-ton steamer into a complete wreck.

The *James Stevens No. 10* was replaced in 1933 by the first motor lifeboat to be stationed at St. Ives, the *Caroline Parsons*, provided by a legacy from Miss Caroline Parsons, of Edinburgh. She arrived on March 18th, having been brought from Cowes by sea, through a terrific 70 m.p.h. gale. During 1936 this boat carried out a notable rescue operation which resulted in awards being made to her crew by the American government. At midnight on November 1st-2nd, the coastguard reported a vessel ashore to the west of St. Ives. She proved to be the steamer *Bessemer City*, of New York, bound for London with general cargo and a crew of thirty-three. She had run on the rocks near Pen Enys Point in a strong N.N.E. breeze with a rough sea. When the lifeboat got alongside the captain refused to leave, but sent ten men aboard the lifeboat, which brought them into St. Ives at 1.45 a.m. At 2.40 a.m. she left again and took off another seventeen, returning with them to St. Ives at 4.50 a.m. After refuelling, she put off a third time to the wreck, which was now breaking up. There was considerable danger in going alongside, as the bow and stern were moving; but, despite this, five officers were rescued, and then, when the ship had broken in two, the captain was taken off. Much of the *Bessemer City*'s cargo, which included many cases of salmon and tinned fruit, washed ashore on Porthmeor Beach, greatly to the profit of the local residents, many of whom still have pleasant memories of this particular shipwreck.

The career of the *Caroline Parsons* came to a tragic close on January 31st 1938, when she was totally wrecked during the first of the two St. Ives lifeboat disasters, which occurred within a year of each other. Just after seven o'clock in the evening, during a severe storm, the 3,700 ton Panamanian steamer *Alba*, bound from Barry to Civita Vecchia, with coal, while attempting to run for shelter in St. Ives Bay, mistook her position in the darkness, and ran aground on the rocks on the north-west side of the Island. The lifeboat was promptly launched, and battled her way through the heavy seas until she came in sight of the steamer. Before getting under the lee of the ship, Coxswain Thomas Cocking ordered the anchor to be dropped and the line paid out, intending to use this when withdrawing from the wreck; but unfortunately, as it happened, the anchor failed to hold. Getting near the *Alba*, the coxswain ordered her crew to get aboard immediately, as the tide was then two hours after ebb, and every moment's delay increased the danger.

Despite this warning, it was six or seven minutes before the men appeared—carrying their effects! Coxswain Cocking ordered them to leave these behind. Heavily laden with twenty-three shipwrecked seamen and her own crew of nine, the lifeboat moved away from the steamer. The seamen were told to lie down on deck, and the *Caroline Parsons* came astern on her engine, the anchor being of no assistance, as a ground swell stirring up the sand made it impossible for the anchor to hold. As the lifeboat cleared the steamer's bow, a tremendous sea struck broadside on, causing her to turn turtle and throwing nearly everyone on board into the sea. Those on shore, including mothers, wives, and other relatives of the lifeboat's crew, stood gazing horror-stricken at this dreadful scene, by the glare of car headlamps, L.S.A. searchlights and hand-torches, and their cry of terror and anguish will never be forgotten by those who heard it. Fortunately, the lifeboat (a self-righter) was on an even keel again in a few seconds.

Coxswain Cocking had been thrown some yards from the boat, but the sea eventually brought him nearer to it, and he was hauled aboard by his son. Some of the steamer's crew, however, were not so fortunate, and nothing could be done to help them, the lifeboat being unmanageable. She then gradually drove ashore until she struck. A line was thrown to her crew by the St. Ives life saving apparatus, and by its aid the men got ashore one after another, being helped over the rocks by hundreds of local people, who braved the rough seas to assist them. Despite the heroic action of the townsfolk, many of whom risked their lives time and time again to snatch the drowning seamen from the water, two were lost, and three brought ashore dead, but all the lifeboatmen were rescued. Coxswain Cocking was subsequently awarded the Silver Medal of the Institution, and the crew Bronze Medals for this heroic rescue; whilst in addition, each man received a monetary award, and an inscribed vellum. The Hungarian Government also presented a Gold Cross of Merit to Coxswain Cocking and a similar award to the Mayor (Mr. C. W. Curnow) in recognition of the gallantry and courage displayed by the townsfolk.

The second lifeboat disaster occurred on January 23rd 1939 and is by far the most tragic event connected with the history of the station. Just before two o'clock on the morning of that fateful day the coast-guards reported a vessel in a dangerous position two miles N.N.E. of Cape Cornwall. A gale of exceptional violence was then raging, with very heavy seas. When it became known at St. Ives that the lifeboat at Sennen Cove could not be launched owing to the tide being low, Coxswain Cocking at once fired the assembly signal. Twenty minutes later the *John and Sarah Eliza Stych*, which had been sent to St. Ives from

The ten-oared Covent Garden *lifeboat of 1870-78 posed on her launching carriage at the edge of St Ives harbour*

The present St Ives lifeboat, Edgar, George, Orlando, & Eva Child *returning from a practice launch. For launching, the submersible Fowler tractor is turned, to push the boat and trailer out into deep water (Photo: Studio St Ives)*

The wreck of the French brigantine Julien Marie *on Porthminster Beach, St Ives, February 5th 1901*

The James Stevens No. 10, *which served for thirty-three years on the St Ives station, taking the crew of three off the schooner* Loango, *May 7th 1909 (Photo: John Behenna)*

Padstow as a replacement for the *Caroline Parsons*, was launched, with the assistance of eighty helpers.

Leaving the shelter of St. Ives Head, the lifeboat at once encountered a very heavy sea. She kept well clear of the headland to avoid the strong flood tide closer in, and turned westward, almost in the teeth of the gale. When about one and a half miles N.N.E. of Clodgy Point the boat sheered as she came down a sea. The following wave struck her on the starboard bow, and she capsized. She was of the self-righting type, and came up again in a few seconds, but four of the eight men on board had been lost—Coxswain Thomas Cocking, William Barber, acting bowman, John Thomas, signalman, and Edgar Bassett. William Freeman, who had been forward, was also thrown into the water, but he kept clear of the gunwale, and two of his comrades dragged him aboard again.

The engine had shut off when the lifeboat capsized, as it was designed to do; but before the motor mechanic could restart it and any attempt be made to pick up the missing men, some of the boat's gear, which had been partly washed out of her, had to be cut away, to avoid fouling the propeller. The mechanic then restarted the engine without difficulty, but when he put in the gear, the engine stalled. He restarted it again, but again it stalled. The astern gear was then engaged and efforts made to clear the propeller, which had fouled despite their precautions. The ahead gear was once more put in, but the engine stalled a third time.

They then dropped their anchor and veered out all the cable. An attempt was made to step the mizzen mast, and with the help of the sail, to keep the lifeboat's head to wind and sea, but with half the boat's complement gone, it proved beyond their power. The lifeboatmen then burned red flares, indicating "More help needed", switched on the searchlight, and burned a white flare. These signals were seen by the coastguard at Clodgy, and the L.S.A. at St. Ives was immediately ordered out to Godrevy Point, on the leeward side of St. Ives Bay, the Portreath apparatus being also summoned from the further side of Godrevy. The Penlee lifeboat was called out at the same time, and launched at five o'clock.

Meanwhile, the lifeboat was sheering about in the terrible seas; and at last the anchor cable parted, although a new one which had never previously been used. The disabled boat now began to drift to leeward across the mouth of the Bay. Several more attempts were made to get the propeller turning again, but each time the engine stalled, and the boat continued drifting helplessly before the storm. Two-thirds of the way across the Bay, a great sea struck her beam on, and she capsized a second time. When she righted, the motor mechanic, Richard Stevens, who was forward, had disappeared.

William Freeman, who was under the canopy above the engine controls, had jammed one hand in the railings below the canopy and grasped the starting handle with the other. When the boat capsized, the pressure of air trapped beneath the canopy kept the water out; even with the keel right above him, he was still able to breathe. Only three survivors now remained on board as the boat continued to drift towards Godrevy, all being aft. As she approached the rocks, Barber, the bowman, then acting as second coxswain, shouted, "Look out, a big sea coming." This wave capsized the boat for the third time. When she righted, only William Freeman remained on board, Barber and the assistant mechanic, John Cocking, having been washed out of her.

Three minutes later, the lifeboat struck the rocks near Godrevy. She was thrown on a fairly level ledge, with her stern towards the shore. As the sea receded, William Freeman crawled out, and made his way on all fours along the rocks. A sea overtook him, but failed to knock him over. He scrambled up a gap in the cliffs, and made his way to Godrevy Farm. Arousing the inhabitants, he poured into their astounded ears the tragic story of that night of death and disaster at sea. Mr. Delbridge, the farmer, thereupon cycled to Hayle to telephone for a doctor to attend the injured man, and also telephoned news of the disaster to the St. Ives Coastguard. It was from this source that the anxiously waiting town heard the first news of this terrible tragedy just after seven o'clock in the morning—news that plunged the whole community into grief and mourning for seven of her bravest sons.

The lifeboat crew included several who had been involved in the previous disaster. Their names were: Thomas Cocking, Coxswain, who had been associated with the lifeboat for 43 years, having held his leading position for eleven of these; R. Q. Stevens, 1st Mechanic; J. B. Cocking, 2nd Mechanic; J. Thomas, Signalman; M. Barber and W. Barber; and W. Bassett and W. Freeman, both volunteers. All were fishermen by calling. Adding to the poignancy of the tragedy was the fact that several of these men were relatives. The two Barbers were brothers and had worked the boat *Our John* for their widowed mother, whilst J. B. Cocking was the son of the Coxswain. Several left widows and small children to mourn their loss. In its long and bitter experience of the sea, St. Ives had rarely known such a catastrophe as this.

Bronze Medals for gallantry were awarded posthumously to all the drowned men by the R.N.L.I., and another to William Freeman, the sole survivor. It was never positively known to what distressed vessel the lifeboat had gone out on that fateful night, but subsequently the wreck of the s.s. *Wilston* (3,000 tons), of and from Glasgow with coal for the Mediterranean, was discovered on the coast at Tregerthen Point, and it seems most likely that she was the ship in question. All 32 people on board were drowned, many of their bodies being recovered in the vicinity of the wreck.

Following this second lifeboat disaster, the St. Ives station was closed; but on the outbreak of hostilities in September 1939 local fishermen pleaded to be allowed to man a new boat, because of the increased danger of wrecks in war-time. The R.N.L.I. acceded to this request, and ordered a boat to be built for the station, which was accordingly re-opened as a temporary war measure in 1940. This lifeboat bore the name *Caroline Oates Aver and William Maine*, being of the light 35 ft. Liverpool type, fitted with a 35 h.p. engine giving a speed of 7 knots, and arrived at St. Ives on January 13th.

She performed her first service on January 21st 1940, being launched with the assistance of many willing helpers who entered the icy water to get her afloat, and searched for two hours in darkness for an aircraft reported in the sea. The 'plane, however, reached base safely. A motor tractor for launching the boat arrived on February 12th; and on that same day the *Maine* was launched for the last time at St. Ives by the old manhandling method, bringing back to the harbour a motor launch which had developed engine trouble near the eastern shores of the Bay. On February 15th a practice launch was effected with the aid of the tractor, which towed the lifeboat on her carriage across the Wharf Road and over the sand to the sea. On reaching the water's edge the tractor was detached from the front and pushed the boat on its carriage into the sea. This system has been used at St. Ives ever since. The original tractor has been replaced by two successive Fowler units of greater power, the latest one, in its dark blue livery, forming a notable feature of the lifeboat station.

The *Caroline Oates Aver and William Maine*, in charge of Coxswain William Peters, carried out valuable work during the Second World War, landing several crews at St. Ives from vessels sunk or damaged by enemy action.

On October 24th 1945, the *Maine* performed a really classic lifeboat rescue when the auxiliary ketch *Minnie Flossie*, of Bideford, was wrecked at Hell's Mouth Cove. At 6.22 a.m. the coastguards reported seeing distress signals from the ketch, which had dragged her anchors, and was drifting across St. Ives Bay. A W.S.W. gale, with heavy squalls of wind and rain, was blowing, and raising a very rough sea. The lifeboat launched at 6.43 and made for Godrevy Island, searching along the shore as she went. She then turned to go outside the Island, and found the ketch at Hell's Mouth Cove, lying on her beam ends close to the shore. There were two people clinging to her, and it seemed the vessel might go under at any moment. The Coxswain knew he must take immediate action, despite the risk involved. Without hesitating, he drove the lifeboat straight at the ketch. At the same moment, however, a heavy sea came in. Lifting the lifeboat, it swept her towards the cliffs, but fortunately receded just as she came abreast the ketch, and the coxswain was able to turn alongside on her weather side, there being insufficient space for this manoeuvre on her lee.

The two people clinging to the vessel—the owner and his wife—were seized by the lifeboatmen and hauled into the boat. The rescue took less than five minutes, and was completed only just in time, for as the lifeboat turned away she met an exceptionally heavy sea, which swept over her, and passing on, completely engulfed the ketch; when the lifeboatmen looked back, she was gone.

In 1948 the *Caroline Oates Aver and William Maine* was replaced by a new lifeboat, the *Edgar, George, Orlando and Eva Child*, a vessel of the Liverpool type, twin-screw, 35 ft. 6 in. in length and 10 ft. 8 in. beam. This boat has performed some excellent services during her career at St. Ives, one of the most remarkable taking place on August 8th 1958. On that day a party of six people, including two children, set out to explore Smuggler's Cave, near Hell's Mouth, Godrevy, hoping to find some seals which frequent this part of the coast. They approached the cave from the landward side by a 300 ft. tunnel and 40 ft. vertical shaft, lowering themselves down without difficulty by means of a rope. When trying to return, however, they found the rope had become wet and slippery; and one of the men, in climbing up, lost his grip, and fell back, striking his head and losing consciousness. Another man thereupon swam out of the cave and attempted to climb the cliff, which rose to a height of 300 ft. After falling back 25 ft. into the sea, he tried again, and this time reached the top, where he was picked up exhausted by a passing motorist. After a telephone message had been sent from a nearby cafe, units of the County Fire Service were sent to the scene from Camborne and Penzance, whilst the St. Ives lifeboat also launched.

Towing a 12 ft. skiff, the boat made her way to Godrevy, directed to the cave by firemen standing on the cliff top. She found it impossible to approach the cave entrance, however, because of the swell and threatening rocks, and Coxswain Daniel Roach decided to send the skiff into the cave with four of the lifeboat's crew of seven—Daniel Paynter, jun. (2nd Coxswain), Jack Paynter (2nd engineer), Martin Roach (third engineer—the Coxswain's son), and Thomas Cocking (bowman). They succeeded in this hazardous venture, but inside the water was swirling about and the sea rising and falling, threatening to smash their skiff against the sides of the cave. Getting out, the lifeboatmen tried to hold the boat to prevent it being damaged, but one minute the sea was just over their ankles and the next up to their necks. At last they could hold the boat no longer, and the heaving water shattered the little craft upon the rocks.

This meant that eight people were now trapped within the cave. It was quite dark inside at times, as when the sea came up it completely covered the entrance, and the lifeboatmen feared they would not get out alive. Daniel Paynter realised the only thing to do was to swim back to the lifeboat to get a line to the cave. He was a strong swimmer, but the heavy seas repeatedly threw him back as he struggled against incoming tide. Meanwhile, those in the lifeboat had not seen or heard anything since the skiff disappeared into the cave, and they waited anxiously outside, tossing about in the swell, wondering what had become of their missing comrades. At last they spotted Daniel Paynter swimming towards them with a lifejacket on, but he experienced great difficulty in reaching the boat, so Michael Peters jumped overboard to fetch him, and he was hauled in after undergoing a gruelling experience. Mr. Paynter expressed a wish to return to the cave with lifejackets, but Coxswain Roach refused to let him try, and Michael Peters then volunteered to go. They gave him a line, and tied all the remaining lifejackets to him, and he then swam off into the cave with 4-500 yards of line, including two rocket lines followed by a heaving line.

The lifeboat then dropped anchor and manoeuvred as near the entrance as she dared. Soon they felt a pull on the rope and started heaving. Michael Peters came out first to keep the rope off the rocks so they could get a straight pull, and the rest of the party followed him "like a string of tin cans", to use the lifeboatmen's own description. There was a lifejacket for each of them, except the little boy, and he hung to the neck of Martin Roach, who was nearly strangled, in consequence. As soon as they were all aboard, the lifeboat raised anchor and made for St. Ives, where hundreds of holidaymakers were waiting to greet her. The lifeboatmen highly praised the spirit of the two children, who remained calm under terrifying circumstances. For this very gallant rescue Motor Mechanic Michael Peters was awarded the Silver Medal of the R.N.L.I., and Coxswain Daniel Roach and Signalman Daniel Paynter a Bronze Medal each, whilst the four other crew members received the Institution's thanks inscribed on vellum.

Of the lifeboat's more recent services, that of the saving of the 259-ton Dieppe trawler *Gai Floreal* and her crew deserves special mention. The trawler, homeward bound with her holds full of fish caught off the south coast of Ireland, missed her bearings and ran aground between Mussel Point and Zennor Cove during the early morning of January 4th 1962, becoming firmly impaled on rocks a hundred yards from the base of the 300 ft. high cliffs. Her skipper put out a distress call, and the lifeboat was launched, whilst the police and coastguards also organised a search of the area. The lifeboatmen found the wreck before daylight, but her skipper refused to abandon ship, so the lifeboat stood by, there being an on-shore wind with a fairly calm sea. Seven members of the crew, including one man who had broken an ankle when the vessel struck, were eventually brought ashore by breeches buoy, but the skipper and eight others preferred to remain on board the trawler, which was holed by a jagged rock near her bows.

There seemed little hope of saving the *Gai Floreal*, but a tug was summoned from Falmouth. Early in the afternoon, however, on the rising tide, the lifeboatmen got a line aboard her, and her engines, which had previously been out of action, were re-started. As the trawler rose on the swell the lifeboat pulled her off the rocks into deep water, and she then proceeded under her own power to St. Ives with the lifeboat in attendance, being berthed in the harbour at 3 p.m. The saving of *Gai Floreal* under these difficult conditions was described by the District Officer of Coastguards as "miraculous", and "a chance in a million".

In common with other lifeboat stations situated in popular holiday resorts, many services are made at St. Ives to assist bathers in distress. The normal type of lifeboat not being too well suited for this class of work, the R.N.L.I. have quite recently introduced a new fast inshore rescue boat (I.R.B.) for use in such emergencies, one of which became operational at St. Ives in May 1964. She is the first of her type in Cornwall. The craft are normally manned by a crew of two, and can be driven at well over 20 knots. This development may be cited as an example of the way in which the Institution is continually seeking to extend and improve its service by adopting the latest technical developments and facilities.

SERVICE RECORD, ST. IVES

Moses (I) Lifeboat

1863	June	12	Schooner *Azores Packet*, of Falmouth, saved	4
	Nov.	11	Pilot Gig of St. Ives, saved gig and	7
1865	Mar.	19	Brigantine *Eclipse*, of St. Ives, saved	2
	Oct.	28	Brigantine *Providence*, of Granville, saved	4
1866	Jan.	11	s.s. *Bessie*, of Hayle, saved	3

Moses (II) Lifeboat (later *Covent Garden* and *Exeter*)

1867	Mar.	17	Schooner *Mary Lewis*, of Aberystwyth, first service, saved	5
			do. second service, gave help	
	Dec.	2	Brig *Courrier du Nord*, of Morlaix, saved	1
1868	Feb.	19	Schooner *Gipsy*, of Chepstow, saved	5
			Pilot Gig, of St. Ives, saved	1
1869	Mar.	20	Schooner *Ariel*, of Truro, saved	5
1871	Feb.	11	Brigantine *Queen*, of Youghal, saved	6
1873	Feb.	2	Schooner *Mary Ann*, of Plymouth, saved	5
			Schooner *Rambler*, of Plymouth, saved	2
			Brig *Francis*, of Swansea, saved	6
1874	Dec.	16	Schooner *Jasper*, of St. Ives, first service, saved	5
			do. second service, assisted to save vessel	
1877	Apr.	17	Dandy *Henri et Helene*, of Nantes, assisted to save vessel	
1878	Mar.	29	Ketch *Greyhound*, of Swansea, assisted to save vessel and	3
1880	Sept.	15	Schooner *Jane Smith*, of Plymouth, saved	6
1881	Jan.	18	Schooner *Rosa Josephs*, of St. Vaast, saved	5
1882	Apr.	29	Lugger *Quick*, of St. Ives, saved	7
			Lugger *Gyles*, of St. Ives, saved	7
			(Also took out fresh crews to these luggers)	
1889	Mar.	21	Ketch *Wave*, of Gloucester, assisted to save vessel	
1890	Dec.	19	Schooner *Secret*, of Penzance, saved	4
1892	Jan.	10	s.s. *Alonso*, of Hull, landed 7	
	July	20	Pilot Cutter *Mary*, of Bristol, saved	4

Reserve No. 7 Lifeboat

1893	Nov.	17	Gig *Boy Philip*, of St. Ives, saved	4
			Gig *Bessie Jane*, of St. Ives, saved	4

Exeter (II) Lifeboat

1895	Jan.	21	Gig *Robert Henry*, of St. Ives, saved	5
			Gig *Children's Friend*, of St. Ives, saved	6
			Gig *Boy Willie*, of St. Ives, accompanied gig to harbour	
	Nov.	25	Lugger *Good Hope*, of St. Ives, stood by	
1896	Mar.	27	Schooner *Lizzie*, of Chester, landed 5	
			Schooner *Laddie*, of St. John's, Newfoundland, landed 7	
	Dec.	4	Ketch *Askelon*, of Jersey, landed 3	
1899	Apr.	21	Lugger *British Workman*, of St. Ives, gave help and landed 7	
	Dec.	1	Gig *Golden Light* and other fishing boats, of St. Ives; rendered assistance	
1900	Nov.	7	Ketch *Star*, of Scilly, saved	3

James Stevens No. 10 Lifeboat

1900	Nov.	6	Escorted fishing vessels to harbour	
		7	Ketch *Foundling*, of Brixham; vessel brought to harbour by a fishing lugger, escorted by lifeboat	
	Dec.	27	Lugger *Honor*, of St. Ives, saved	5
1901	Feb.	5	Brigantine *Julien Marie*, of Auray, saved a dog and	6
1903	Sept.	11	Schooner *Enterprise*, of Beaumaris, saved	4
1906	Dec.	12	Barquentine *Try Again*, of Padstow, landed 5	
1907	Oct.	17	Schooner *Susan Elizabeth*, of St. Ives; saved	4
1908	Jan.	7	Schooner *Lizzie R. Wilce*, of Falmouth, saved	5
		8	Schooner *Mary Barrow*, of Barrow, saved	5
		28	Ketch *Ystwyth*, of Padstow, saved	3
			Trawler *Victor*, of Brixham, landed 4	
	Mar.	6	Ketch *Charles Francis*, of Scilly, saved	3
1909	May	7	Schooner *Loango*, of Sligo, saved	3
	Dec.	1	s.s. *Congress*, of Liverpool, saved	1
1910	May	12	Lugger *Jonadab*, of St. Ives, saved	6
1911	Jan.	11	Lugger *Ripple*, of St. Ives, accompanied vessel to harbour	
1913	Mar.	17	Schooner *St. Clair*, of Plymouth, landed 6 and a dog	
	Apr.	24	s.s. *Othon Stathatos*, of Ithaca, saved	23
			do. assisted to save vessel	
1915	Dec.	27	s.s. *Taunton*, of Liverpool, saved	9
		28	do. assisted to save vessel	
1917	Jan.	10	Schooner *Lottie*, of Padstow, saved a dog and	5
		31	s.s. *Dundee*, of Hamilton, Ontario; vessel torpedoed about 6 miles N. of St. Ives Head; lifeboat found floating wreckage; steamer's crew saved by patrol boat	
	Oct.	10	s.s. *Seapoint*, of London, saved vessel and	15
	Dec.	2	Boats of Transport *Kintuck*, of Liverpool, saved	34
1918	May	2	s.s. *Norlands*, of Tonsberg, saved	17
1920	Jan.	2	s.s. *Valur*, of Reykjavik, saved vessel and	14
1921	July	29	Ketch *H. F. Bolt*, of Bideford, saved	3
			Ketch *Anne*, of Gloucester, saved	4
			Crab-boat *St. Eloi*, of Camaret, saved	5
			Crab-boats *Suzanne Yvonne*, *St. Mauday* and *Eclair*, of Camaret, saved	12
			Crab-boats *Turquoise*, of Camaret; *Anne Marie*, *En Avant*, and *Providence*, of Paimpol, saved	16
1922	Dec.	22	s.s. *Eleanor*, of London, saved	16
1923	Feb.	6	Motor schooner *Elsie*, of Swansea, landed 4 and gave help	
		22	Schooner *Mary Jones*, of Chester, gave help and landed 4	
	Dec.	25	Fishing boat *Peggy*, of St. Ives, helped to save vessel and	5
1925	Dec.	25	Landed a sick keeper from Godrevy Lighthouse	
1929	May	6	Motor fishing boat *Our Girls*, of St. Ives, escorted boat to safety	
	Dec.	7	Ketch *St. Austell*, of Barnstaple, landed 2 and a dog	
1930	Nov.	6	Ketch *Dido C.*, of Barnstaple, landed 3	

Caroline Parsons Lifeboat

1933	June	8	Motor boat *White Heather*, of St. Agnes, saved boat and	3
1936	June	13	Ketch *St. Austell*, of Barnstaple, saved vessel and	4
	Nov.	2	s.s. *Bessemer City*, of New York, saved (in 3 trips)	33
			do. fourth trip, took master to wreck	
1937	July	1	s.s. *Aida Lauro*, of Naples, saved	15
1938	Jan.	31	s.s. *Alba*, of Panama; lifeboat wrecked; saved	18

John and Sarah Eliza Stych Lifeboat

1938	Aug.	16	Rowing boat *Boy Sam*, of Falmouth (at Falmouth) saved boat and	1
1939	Jan.	23	s.s. *Wilston*, of Glasgow; lifeboat wrecked	

Caroline Oates Aver and William Maine Lifeboat

1940	Feb.	12	Admiralty Motor Cruiser *East Mora*, saved cruiser and	4
1941	Feb.	1	s.s. *Kia*, of Gloucester, landed 10, recovered a body and ship's boat	
	Apr.	16	s.s. *Amiens*, of Swansea, landed 2 injured men	
		23	British "Hurricane" Aircraft, landed a body	
	May	8	H.M.S. *Viva II*, rendered assistance and landed 5	
		23	s.s. *Bidassoa*, of Falmouth, escorted to safety	
1943	Aug.	25	Dinghy of "Anson" Aircraft, saved	5
	Nov.	15	m.v. *Teasel*, of Cardiff, gave help and stood by	
	Dec.	2	m.v. *Reiger*, of Zuidbroek, landed 1	
1944	Oct.	11	U.S. Navy tugs LT.23 and LT.61, with floating cranes, stood by	
1945	Apr.	23	s.s. *Riverton*, of Newcastle, landed 34	
	July	27	s.s. *David L. Swain*, of Wilmington, N.C., landed sick man	
		31	H.M.S. *Grenadier*, landed a sick man	
	Oct.	24	Motor ketch *Minnie Flossie*, of Bideford, saved	2
1946	Feb.	6	s.s. *Jellicoe Rose*, of Liverpool, saved	12
		9	do. gave help	
	Mar.	19	Boat of m.v. *Wilja*, of Groningen, saved boat and	3
1947	May	2	Motor Boat *Entente Cordiale*, landed 8	
	June	12	Auxiliary Yacht *Fubbs*, of Southampton, gave help	

Edgar, George, Orlando and Eva Child Lifeboat

1948	Sept.	4	s.s. *Moyallon*, of Belfast, landed an injured man	
1949	July	26	Motor Boat *Reaper*, of St. Ives, gave help	
	Sept.	25	Two small boats, saved two boats and	6
1950	May	31	m.v. *Sand Runner*, of Goole, gave help	
	July	2	Landed the body of a bather	
1952	Mar.	8	Tanker *British Diligence*, of London, landed an injured man	
	Apr.	24	s.s. *Rocquaine*, of Guernsey, landed an injured man	
1953	Aug.	9	Motor Yacht *Totland*, towed to safe position	
1955	June	18	Motor Yacht *Molin*, of Guernsey, towed yacht to harbour	
	Aug.	22	Fishing Boat *Dido*, of Portreath, saved boat and	3
1956	July	15	Skiff *Tregenna Castle*, of St. Ives, landed 1	
	Sept.	16	M. Tug *Amcotts*, of Forcados, saved tug and	8

Frank and William Oates (Reserve) Lifeboat

1958	Mar.	14	Boat of m.v. *Erkalin*, of Groningen, put boat and man on board	

Edgar, George, Orlando and Eva Child Lifeboat

1958	June	25	Fishing Boat *May*, of St. Ives, saved boat and	2
	July	14	Fishing Boat *Doris*, of St. Ives, saved boat and	1
	Aug.	9	Party cut off in cave, saved	4
	Nov.	18	Motor Launch *Shaiba*, saved launch and	4
	Dec.	20	Trawler *Autumn Sun*, of Yarmouth, escorted vessel to harbour	
1959	Feb.	8	m.v. *Flevo*, of Groningen, escorted vessel to harbour	
	Apr.	18	m.v. *Marjan*, of Waalwijk, assisted to save vessel	

Frank and William Oates (Reserve) Lifeboat

1959	Aug.	6	m.v. *Kindrence*, of Rochester, took out a doctor	

Edgar, George, Orlando and Eva Child Lifeboat

1959	Aug.	17	M. Yacht *Taiseer V.*, of Southampton, refloated yacht and escorted to harbour	
	Sept.	3	m.v. *Crescence*, of Rochester, stood by until refloated	
1961	May	25	Fishing Boat *White Heather*, of St. Ives, saved boat and	4
	June	28	Motor Fishing Skiff *Our John*, of St. Ives, landed 1	
	Aug.	26	Two men trapped on cliffs, stood by while saved from land	

1962	Jan.	4	M. Trawler *Gai Floreal*, of Dieppe, saved trawler and	9
	Feb.	18	Two men trapped in a cave, stood by while saved from land	
	July	20	M. Yacht *Liana*, of Southampton, saved yacht and	3
1963	June	12	M. Trawler *Etoile D'Arvor*, of Audierne, towed trawler to safety	
	Nov.	26	m.v. *Arthur Albright*, of London, landed a sick man	

BOAT RECORD, ST. IVES

Years on Station	Length, Breadth, Depth	Type, Oars, Crew	Weight, Cost, O. No.	Built Year, Builder	Boat's Name, Donor, Authority
1840-1861	30′ 5′ 9″ 2′ 3″	 8 10	 £150 —	1840 Fras. J. Adams, St. Ives	*Hope* Local Subscriptions Local Committee
1861-1866	30′ 7′ 3′ 3″	Peake 6 9	1t10 £157 —	1860 Forrestt, Limehouse	*Moses* Anon. lady, Co. Durham R.N.L.I.
1866-1886	32′ 7′ 6″ 3′ 6″	SR 10 13	 £259 —	1866 Forrestt, Limehouse	*Moses*[1] As above R.N.L.I.
1886-1901	34′ 7′ 6″	SR 10 13	 £296 50	1886[2] Woolfe, Shadwell	*Exeter* Leg. Wm. Kendall, Exeter R.N.L.I.
1900-1933	37′ 6″ 9′ 3″	SR 12 15	4t11 £834 435	1899 Thames Ironworks, Blackwall	*James Stevens No. 10* Leg. Mr. Jas. Stevens, [Birmingham R.N.L.I.
1933-1938	35′ 6″ 9′ 3″	SR(M) — 7	7t £3215 763	1933 White & Co. Cowes	*Caroline Parsons* Leg. Miss C. Parsons, [Edinburgh R.N.L.I.
1938-1939	35′ 6″ 8′ 10″	SR(M) — 7	6t £5754 743	1931[3] Saunders Roe, Cowes	*John and Sarah Eliza Stych* Legs. Mr. & Mrs. Jn. Stych, [Birmingham R.N.L.I.
1940-1948	35′ 6″ 10′ 3″	L(M) — 7	6t14 £4289 831	1939[4] Groves & G., E. Cowes	*Caroline Oates Aver & William Maine* Legs. Mrs. C. Aver, Penryn, & Miss C. L. Maine, [Clapton R.N.L.I.

1948-	35′ 6″ 10′ 8″	L(M) — 7	8t14 £9752 861	1948 Groves & Guttridge E. Cowes	*Edgar, George, Orlando & Eva Child* Legs. Mr. R. B. Pole, London, M. O. F. Child, Hereford, Maj. G. Wilson, Lewisham & Miss L. E. Cockroft R.N.L.I.

1 1870 renamed *Covent Garden*, for the Covent Garden Lifeboat Fund
1878 renamed *Exeter*, for the legacy of Wm. Kendal, Exeter.

2 Altered and improved 1893-4.

3 Formerly stationed at Padstow.

4 Transferred to Ferryside, Wales, in 1948.

SENNEN COVE

THE LAND'S END of England bears a strangely ambivalent reputation. To the landsman it is Bolerium, the romantic westernmost tip of Britain, that far-famed "narrow neck of land" set amid romantic, awe-inspiring cliff scenery with incomparable views seawards to the Longships and the Atlantic Ocean, and haunted by memories of the lost land of Lyonesse, Scilly. To the sailor, however, its name carries a dread of hidden reefs, dangerous tide races, confused cross seas, and an iron-bound coastline where many a proud and well-found vessel has met a violent end.

The shipwreck which, above all others, drew attention to the urgent need for establishing a lifeboat in this area proved also the occasion of a truly heroic rescue operation—one of the most gallant ever seen in this county. This took place on January 11th 1851, when the *New Commercial* (a brig—or more correctly, snow—of 250 tons, registered at Whitby) struck on a ledge connecting the Great and Little Brisons—those two fearful rocks which thrust their sharp fangs out of the sea about a mile south-west of Cape Cornwall. There was a thick fog at the time with seas running very high, and the vessel went to pieces almost immediately. The crew of nine and the master's wife reached the ledge, their plight being discovered from shore when day broke, but no assistance could possibly be given them. About nine o'clock, however, all the survivors were swept away by a tremendous wave, and seven of them drowned. Of the three who scrambled back, one, a mulatto called Isaac Williams, contrived to get on a piece of floating spar; using a plank for a paddle and a piece of canvas for a sail, he managed, with great coolness and presence of mind, and assisted by the tide, to get clear of the Brisons and pilot his frail craft into Whitesand Bay. After beating about here for some hours he was rescued by William Roberts and four Sennen fishermen who bravely launched their boat *Grace* through the breakers. The two others who regained the rock were Capt. and Mrs. Sanderson, both being washed on to the Little Brison.

Meanwhile, Capt. George Davies, R.N., Inspecting Commander of the Coastguard at Penzance, ordered the revenue cruiser *Sylvia* round the Land's End, whilst he, with Lieut. Maxey, R.N., of the Sennen Coastguard, and Mr. Paule, of Pendeen, took up positions on Cape Cornwall. The *Sylvia* gallantly worked her way round the Longships, her topmast at times being completely hidden by flying spray. On coming abreast of the Cape, Mr. Forward launched a boat and with four men tried to get near the rock. But the endeavour was hopeless, and they only regained the cutter with great difficulty. Darkness was now falling, and nothing further could be done till the following morning. Mr. Forward, however, hoisted his colours and hove to, to give encouragement to the two survivors. With daylight the wind fortunately veered a little to the S.E., which caused the seas to abate; and at one o'clock four boats could be seen approaching from Sennen, one manned by the Coastguard and the other three by local fishermen.

At the same time Capt. Davies appeared in charge of a Preventive boat from Pendeen, manned by four Preventive men and one miner, whilst the cutter's boat was again launched, in charge of Mr. Forward, making six rescue boats on the scene altogether. They were cheered on in their attempt by the crowds on the cliffs, which had now grown to between 5-6,000 people, but the sea ran so high that no boat could venture within a hundred yards of the Brisons.

Capt. Davies, however, had brought in his boat (measuring only 25 ft. by 6 ft.) several 9-pounder Dennett rockets which had never before been used by the local coastguard either from the shore or a boat. According to the printed instructions, the person firing should be several feet to the rear to avoid danger. Gunner Selley volunteered for this task, but Capt. Davies decided to attempt it himself. He put his crew in a Sennen boat, fixed the triangle in position, placed another boat astern to train his own and fired the rocket. For an instant he was enveloped in flame but sustained no injury. The line, unfortunately, fell on a sharp ledge, was cut, and slipped back into the sea. The second line fell close to the master, and as if to bring encouragement at this critical moment the sun shone through brilliantly, spotlighting the two lonely figures on the Little Brison. Capt. Sanderson fastened the line round his wife's waist, and urged her to jump into the water. She hesitated, fearing the awful leap, but encouraged by his persuasions, at last sprang into the sea, clad only in her white nightclothes. But what all hoped would prove a spring to safety, became a leap into the jaws of death; for at this moment three immense waves broke in rapid succession, imperilling the safety of all. The boats were completely hidden from view, and a great cry went up from the thousands of spectators: "They are gone!".

The waves passed, however, leaving the boats unscathed, and within three minutes Mrs. Sanderson was drawn from the water, but so exhausted that she died before reaching shore. The Captain was pulled to another boat and all were landed at Sennen, the bodies of Mrs. Sanderson and several members of the crew being later buried in the churchyard there.

Soon after this, Capt. Davies was appointed Inspector of Lifeboats to the R.N.L.I. He had a long record of lifesaving, being personally involved in rescuing two hundred persons. For his gallant work in connection with the *New Commercial* he was given that most coveted award, the Gold Medal of the R.N.L.I., a similar distinction being granted to Mr. Forward of the *Sylvia.* Silver Medals were awarded to the following: Gunner Charles S. Carr, James Richards, William Surrey, Henry Jones, Henry Richards, mariners; 1st class boy James Ward of the *Sylvia*; Cd. Btmn. James Burne; Btmn. Thomas Kerley; Btmn. Robert Eastaway; Cd. Btmn. William Henry Selley, Coastguard Sennen. Rewards were also made to a miner, John Thomas; William Roberts and four men of the *Grace* of Sennen Cove; and Samuel Nicholas and four men of the *Two Brothers* of Sennen Cove.

This epic rescue brought much glory to the little fishing village of Sennen Cove, nestling beneath the high cliffs on Whitesand Bay about a mile north of Land's End. The noble and fearless conduct of its people was rewarded not only with medals, prized though these must have been, but by their being given more effective means of displaying their courage at like shipwrecks in the future. For at their Annual General Meeting on April 22nd 1852, the National Shipwreck Institution stated that an eight-oared Peake-type lifeboat, built by Wallis, was ready for despatch to Sennen "in acknowledgement of the gallant conduct of the Coast Guards and fishermen of that place on the occasion of the wreck of the ship *New Commercial* on the Brisons."

This boat, however, was not forwarded, it being subsequently decided that a lighter one would be more suitable for the station. So, another lifeboat, measuring 25 ft. 8 in. by 6 ft. 10 in., also of Peake design, but built by Forrestt of Limehouse, and rowing six oars, arrived at Sennen in June 1853, being conveyed to Penzance in the British and Irish Steam Packet Co's. steamer and from there towed to its destination by the local revenue cruiser. A stone boathouse, measuring 28 ft. by 12 ft., had been built at Sennen the previous year at the sole expense of James Trembath, Esq., of Mayon House; this building stood on the site of the present one. In 1856 a carriage was ordered for the station to assist in the launching, which always presented great difficulties.

This lifeboat's first and only service took place on May 6th and 7th 1856, when, with some shore boats, she brought the abandoned barque *Charles Adolphe*, of La Rochelle, into Penzance. This vessel had been in collision in a S.E. gale off Land's End, and £100 was awarded to the Sennen lifeboat for her part in this operation. After a fifth of this had been deducted for the maintenance of the boat (in accordance with the Institution's rules) each of the eight lifeboatmen received only about £8 or £9 each—a decision which led the local secretary (Mr. Trembath) to lodge an unsuccessful appeal at headquarters. It was pointed out to him that this amount considerably exceeded the normal £1 service money, and that the men had not incurred risk with their own lives or property.

In July 1864 this lifeboat was replaced by the *Cousins William and Mary Ann of Bideford*, presented by Mrs. Mary Ann Davis of Bideford. A larger boat than its predecessor, it rowed ten oars, and was of the self-righting type. The boathouse had to be altered to acccommodate it, this work costing £80 5s.

The *Cousins* performed her first service on October 13th 1865, when she put off in answer to signals of distress from the Longships lighthouse, and brought ashore in heavy seas one of the lightkeepers, who was seriously ill. Her most outstanding service took place three years after this, on October 23rd 1868. Soon after two o'clock that morning, the look-out on board the Government lighter *Devon*, rounding Land's End en route from Devonport for Queenstown, with stores, gave the alarm that two ships were riding off, without lights, These "ships", however, were the dreaded Brisons; and soon realising his mistake, the man changed his cry to "Rocks! Breakers! Rocks!" but all efforts by the master and crew to avoid the inevitable disaster failed. In the rain and darkness of that wild autumn night the *Devon* ran stern first on to the Brisons, and within a quarter of an hour had completely broken in pieces.

Whilst there was yet time, the boats were lowered, but the heavy seas immediately swept them away; and of the eighteen persons on board the lighter, seventeen, including the Captain, a woman and two children passengers, lost their lives in this appalling tragedy. Only one man survived the buffeting among the rocks and wreckage—the mate. He owed his preservation to the fact that he jumped boldly to seaward from the disintegrating ship, thus avoiding the seething waters between her and the rocks, where others had been instantly killed, and was eventually flung up by the sea completely exhausted into a cleft on the lesser island. Early next morning portions of the wreck were discerned from shore, and the coastguard stationed at St. Just observed the mate moving in the nook where he had taken refuge. Coxswain Matthew Nicholas assembled the lifeboat crew, and they pulled through a heavy cross sea to the Brisons where as the boat tumbled about for forty-five minutes in the rough seas, those on board shouted themselves hoarse to try and attract the castaway's attention. Getting no answer, they were about to give up in despair and return, when Davis moved his position, and was sighted by his rescuers at the moment he first saw them.

He wanted to plunge in immediately, but was stopped, as many rocks lay nearby. Mr. Sylvester Morrison, Chief Coastguard Officer at Sennen, had joined the lifeboat crew with the rocket apparatus; and when they had anchored about 180 yards to the leeward of the rocks this was prepared for firing as in the *New Commercial* rescue seventeen years before. The stand for the rocket tube proved too high, so it was lashed fore-and-aft in the lifeboat. The first line went over the rock near Davis, and he hauled it in slowly, being weak from exposure. He then hauled a buoy over, and in this was dragged to the lifeboat half insensible from cold and exposure. The R.N.L.I. awarded Silver Medals to Coxswain Matthew Nicholas and Chief Officer (2nd Class) Sylvester Morrison, of the Coastguard, for their brave conduct.

The Sennen lifeboat which performed so well on this occasion achieved some equally notable successes in her "off-duty" moments. It was, at that period, the practice to hold "lifeboat races" at various regattas in west Cornwall; and the *Cousins* of Sennen appears to have won the majority of them. The most celebrated of these races took place at Penzance in 1867 and 1869, Sennen taking first place in both (see Penzance). Others followed at Hayle Pool in 1870 and 1872.

A new lifeboat house was erected at Sennen in 1875 at a cost of £258. This building is still in existence, being on the landward side of the road leading to the harbour, a few yards east of the present house. Five years later (August 1880) a new lifeboat was also provided, the existing one having received extensive damage at different times. Presented by Miss Maria Onslow of Staughton House, St. Neot, in memory of her brother, this was named *Denzil and Maria Onslow*. Measuring 34 ft. by 8 ft. 3 in.,

A silent crowd watches the fishery protection vessel H.M.S. Wave, *her stern close under Westcot's Quay, St Ives, October 30th 1952. Note the breeches-buoy line (Photo: Studio St Ives)*

The Lizzie R. Wilce *(foreground) and the* Mary Barrow, *ashore on Porthminster Beach, January 8th 1908. Both were well-known west-country schooners, built on the Fal. The former was never got off but the* Mary Barrow *was repaired and was finally wrecked in 1938 on the Isle of Man (Photo: Gibson)*

The steamer Alba, *beginning to break up, January 31st 1938. The seas were much rougher than this when the lifeboat came round the bow and waited to pick up the crew in the lee of the bridge (Photo: Studio St Ives)*

The battered remains of the Caroline Parsons *on the rocks at Porthmeor, the day following the first St Ives lifeboat disaster in 1938 (Photo: Studio St Ives)*

The funeral pyre of the John and Sarah Eliza Stych *at Godrevy, January 1939. She was smashed beyond repair and after removal of her engine and fittings, she was burnt—like the* Caroline Parsons—*by order of the local Committee rather than leave her to predatory souvenir hunters (Photo: Studio St Ives)*

The two halves of the American steamship Bessemer City *(5686 tons) after she had struck on Pen Enys Point, west of St Ives, November 2nd 1936*

The schooner Mildred, *of Padstow, half-submerged near Gurnard's Head, Zennor, 1912 (Photo: Gibson)*

The full-rigged ship Alexander Yeats *at Gurnard's Head, September 25th 1896. She was bound from Georgia to Devonport with timber and went ashore here in fog*

it rowed ten oars double-banked, and cost £363. This lifeboat was publicly launched at Penzance on August 20th, the occasion of the annual swimming races, when she also took part in a friendly contest with the Penzance boat.

On the afternoon of January 8th 1883, the cutter *Spring*, of Guernsey, bound from Swansea for Dinan with coal was sighted by the Sennen coastguard flying a distress signal at 1.30 p.m. Whilst beating in to come to an anchor in Whitesand Bay she had been run into by an unknown schooner, carrying away her jibboom and part of her stem and causing her to leak very badly. It was blowing a fearful gale from the S.E. at the time, and the smack's crew of three gladly welcomed the lifeboat's arrival on the scene. Chief Officer Steed, of the Coastguard, who was in charge of the lifeboat in the absence of the regular Coxswain, boarded the *Spring* with two of his crew and anchored her in a safe place about four miles out. The lifeboat then took off the *Spring*'s crew and landed them at Sennen. This was a very arduous service, lasting four and a half hours, the lifeboatmen, who were drenched to the skin, suffering severely from the cold.

The s.s. *Malta*, of Glasgow, bound from Liverpool for Italy with passengers and general cargo, went ashore at Wheal Castle, about four miles from Sennen, in a dense fog on the evening of October 15th 1889. The lifeboat was launched at 8.30 p.m., and found the passengers had been landed, but stood by at the master's request. An attempt to tow her off on the following day failed, and the steamer later settled and became a total wreck, the master and six men being taken off by lifeboat, the rest landing in their own boats. The R.N.L.I. awarded its Thanks on Vellum to Edward and William Roberts of St. Just for their help in landing passengers from the *Malta*. A reward of £5 was also made to two others for saving, at very great risk, six of the seven men in a boat from the steamer which was capsized by an enormous wave when returning to shore with salvaged property on October 16th.

On September 30th 1891, the keepers on the Longships signalled that a schooner was in distress. A severe gale prevailed at the time with high seas breaking in the Cove; and when Coxswain Nicholas arrived a number of the crew refused to go out in such conditions. He then called for volunteers, and seven of the normal thirteen came forward, together with five others, mostly holiday visitors. They launched, and could see the schooner's flares off the Brisons, but these disappeared before they reached the spot. The vessel—the *Annie Davies*, of Caernarvon—was found abandoned the following day in the Bristol

Channel by the s.s. *Gazelle*, her crew having apparently taken to the boats, which were swamped in the gale. The lifeboat searched for her for two hours, but the wind then increased to hurricane force, making it impossible to return to Sennen. Accordingly the boat made for St. Ives, which they reached the following morning after four hours hard rowing. Volunteers forming the crew—Frank Bodilly, barrister; Thomas L. Burgwin, stockbroker, and H. J. Welch, artist—were awarded the Institution's Thanks on Vellum for their courageous action.

In 1893 a new lifeboat arrived at Sennen. Named the *Ann Newbon*, she measured 35 ft. by 8 ft. 3in., rowing ten oars. Soon after this (in 1894-6) a large boathouse, with slipway and separate carriage house was built on the site of the original house of 1852. This improvement cost £1680, plus £325 for a new road to Whitesand Bay.

The *Ann Newbon*'s first service took place on Christmas Eve 1894, when H.M.S. *Lynx* struck the rocks off Sennen Cove in dense fog at about 8 p.m. She successfully backed off and brought up in deep water, but at the Commander's request the lifeboat stood by all night. When the fog cleared at about 5.30 the following morning, the lifeboat helped to raise the warship's anchor, her capstan having been carried away. The *Lynx* then proceeded with the *Ann Newbon* in tow and the Coxswain piloting for a distance of twelve miles. As the warship was not leaking as badly as feared, she went on to Devonport, the lifeboat returning to her station.

A remarkable shipwreck took place at about midnight on November 9th 1898 when the s.s. *Blue Jacket*, of Cardiff, bound from Plymouth for her home port in ballast, with a crew of 22, struck hard and fast on the rocks under the Longships lighthouse in clear weather. The Assistant Coxswain was fishing off Cape Cornwall when his attention was drawn to signals from the lighthouse; he returned to Sennen, and roused the Coxswain, the lifeboat being launched at 1.05 a.m. She reached the scene of the wreck within twenty minutes of summoning the crew, and found that four of the steamer's boats had already been launched. One of these had been stove and two contained the men's effects. The crew decided to land, so they got on board, and towing the laden boats arrived at Sennen after three hours strong pulling against a very strong tide. The steamer became a total wreck.

On October 21st 1901, the *Ann Newbon* landed five men from two fishing boats who were in difficulties in a high sea; and on November 18th she saved the crew of six of the schooner *Mary James*, of Penzance, bound from Newlyn to Swansea with copper ore and stone, which foundered close to the Brisons in a strong N.W. gale. This vessel had been engaged principally by the Levant mine carrying copper ore and coal, and was well known in west Cornwall.

An effective illustration of the old adage that "good sometimes comes out of evil" was provided by a most dreadful shipwreck which occurred in this area on February 15th 1905. On that day, the ship *Khyber*, of Liverpool, homeward bound from Australia, anchored in a distressed condition off Land's End during a terrible gale, her crew taking to the rigging. News of her plight reached Sennen, but the lifeboat could not get away from the slip, the seas being head on. Her carriage, which had been removed the previous year as unnecessary, might have proved useful on this occasion. The *Khyber* eventually came ashore at Porthloe Cove, and soon broke up, only three of the 26 on board being saved through the efforts of watchers on shore.[1] At a subsequent B.o.T. enquiry, it was recommended that a breakwater be built to protect the lifeboat's launching place, and this was in due course erected, its cost being defrayed by voluntary contributions, principally through the exertions of Col. H. W. Williams, of St. Ives.

A happier fate than that of the *Khyber* befell the full-rigged ship *Fairport*, of Liverpool, which, on the evening of December 29th 1908 was observed anchored close inshore in Porthcurno Bay during a whole southerly gale. Her anchors held until five o'clock the following morning when she commenced to drag towards Logan Rock. Two hours later, with the weather moderating, the tug *Blazer*, which had been accompanying the *Fairport*, arrived with the salvage vessel *Lady of the Isles* from Penzance, and stood by for some time until the vessel slipped and buoyed her anchors, the tug then towing her away in an easterly direction. The Sennen lifeboat rendered invaluable assistance on this occasion, As soon as the Coxswain had been informed by phone of the ship's plight, she was launched, but when within half a mile of the Longships they found it impossible to make any headway against the wind and sea, and returned to Sennen. At three a.m., however, the wind shifted, and they set out again, but it soon changed again to W.S.W., throwing up a tremendous sea, the waves running mountains high. From the lighthouse to Porthcurno the boat could carry only a close-reefed foresail, and at times she was swept by the

1. Penzance lifeboat made a gallant attempt to save the *Khyber*'s crew. With such a terrific head wind, it was not possible for her to sail to the scene, but the salvage steamer *Lady of the Isles* towed the boat to Porthloe. They arrived about eleven o'clock, the lifeboat shipping water all the way, only to find that the vessel had already foundered.

following seas which filled her to the gunwale. Rain was also falling in sheets, and the night pitch dark. Soon after daylight they fetched into Porthcurno Bay, and brought her alongside the *Fairport*, where they stood by. Soon after the *Fairport* slipped her anchors and was towed away. The *Ann Newbon* made for home, but heavy wind and sea obliged the Coxswain to run for Penzance instead. Coxswain Henry Nicholas received the Institution's Silver Medal for this fine service, which resulted in the saving of the ship and her crew of nineteen. Newlyn lifeboat also launched on this occasion, but failed to find the *Fairport*.

The Sennen boat went again to Porthcurno on March 13th 1910, when the Brixham trawler *Harry* stranded when on its way to the fishing grounds and rapidly became a wreck. In answer to flares seen by the coastguard at 2.45 a.m. she put out and found a small boat containing four men, which was towed back to Sennen through a heavy gale. Another Brixham trawler, the *Condor*, was in trouble near Land's End on March 14th 1912, in heavy seas, and the lifeboat stood by until a change of wind enabled her to get clear. She also stood by the ketch *Woolwich Infant*, of Falmouth, which parted her cable and drifted rapidly towards Cowloe Rocks in a moderate E.N.E. gale on April 4th 1913. The ketch managed to re-anchor near the rocks, and the lifeboat returned to station. Later, however, the *Woolwich Infant* drove ashore and became a total loss, her crew being rescued by a shore boat before the lifeboat could reach her again. On August 14th of that same year she saved two men from the steamship *J. Duncan*, of Cardiff, bound from Cardiff to Devonport with coal, which stranded at Tol Pedn Penwith in thick fog, and towed three ship's boats with the rest of the crew to Porthgwarra Cove.

The *Ann Newbon* performed several useful services during the First World War. On April 21st 1917 she saved the Captain and six men from the s.s. *Polyktor*, of Ithaca, aground at Pendeen, laden with coal, and towed ashore the remaining 21 crew members in the ship's boats. On September 10th that year the s.s. *Ioanna*, of London, was torpedoed by submarine off the Longships; a patrol boat took off the crew, but two wounded men and a boy were sent ashore by lifeboat, the steamer being towed to port. On February 7th 1918 the s.s. *Beaumaris*, also of London, was torpedoed 2½ miles N.W. of the Longships, the lifeboat going out to help as she came shorewards. They piloted her until she grounded, and some lifeboatmen then assisted in letting go her anchors, the Captain and a wireless operator being the only persons on board.

A boat, with the rest of the crew, numbering 18, had abandoned ship about two miles out, so the lifeboat made a search and brought them in.

On March 17th 1919 the motor fishing vessel *Ben-ma-Chree*, whilst on her way to the fishing grounds from Newlyn, met a boat from the Falmouth steamer *Falmouth Castle* which had been beached by her captain after striking the Lee Ore Reef between the Runnelstone and Land's End. Seven men in her were transferred to the fishing boat. The Sennen lifeboat launched to the steamer's assistance, and falling in with the *Ben-ma-Chree*, took off the survivors for landing at Penzance. The rest of the crew were taken off by Porthcurno rocket apparatus, whilst the captain's wife, an elderly lady, was saved by Alfred Jackson of Porthgwarra in his 14 ft punt with considerable difficulty amid the heavy seas, a feat which earned him the Silver Medal of the R.N.L.I.

The s.s. *Frisia*, of Rotterdam, bound from Cardiff for Rouen with coal, became uncontrollable in a whole N.N.E. gale during the afternoon of April 29th 1919 to the N.W. of the Brisons. She had so heavy a list that her bridge was in the water, and the *Ann Newbon* put off to her. During the evening the steamer foundered about half a mile N.W. of Ayr Point when the lifeboat was only about 200 yards away. The crew of fourteen, who had left in their boat, were transferred and landed at Sennen.

In 1919 extensive alterations had been put in hand to make the station suitable for a motor lifeboat, including the laying of a trolley-way down the slip. The first motor lifeboat, named *The Newbons*, a 40 ft self-righter, arrived at Sennen on May 1st 1922. Having left Cowes (in company with the new Appledore lifeboat) on April 28th she covered the 226 miles in 30 hours at an average speed of 7½ knots. The inaugural ceremony was held on August 28th 1924.

Her first service took place on September 29th 1923, when the steamer *Gutfeld*, of Hamburg, bound from London to Cardiff, ran aground near Cape Cornwall in thick fog. The Coxswain went aboard, and under his direction she got clear of the reef and proceeded to Falmouth for repairs. Soon after this the s.s. *City of Westminster*, a fine vessel of 6,000 tons gross, bound from Belfast for Rotterdam with maize, and having 73 persons on board, struck the Runnelstone in thick weather on the top of the tide, and remained fast on the rocks. The lifeboat reached her at 11 a.m. and took off three women and ten of the crew, an operation rendered difficult by the rise and fall of the sea. Twenty-five of the crew who took to two of the ship's boats were towed to port by the Penzance steam drifter *Pioneer*, whilst the Penlee lifeboat saved

Carn Naun Pt
Pen Enys Pt
The Carracks
Wicca Pool
Treveal
Trevalgan
Carlow Rocks
Trevega
Zennor Hd
Wicca
Trendrine
Pendour Cove
Tremeader
Tregerthen
Gurnard's Head
Zennor
Trereen Dinas
Carnellow
Towednack
C.G.Sta.
Boswednack
Porthmeor
Trereen
Inn
Trewey Hill
Foage
Amalveor Downs
Amalveor
Amalwhidden
Porthmeor
Porthmorna
Bosigran
Brandys
Rosemergy
Bosporthennis
Tumuli
Lady Downs
Amalebrea
Three Stone Oar
Carn Galva
Hannibals Carn
Bishops Head & Foot
Lighthouse
Pendeen Watch
Portheras Cove
Carn Clough
Morvah
Watch Croft
Mulfra Hill
Mulfra Quoit
Pendeen
Trevean
Kerrow Hill
Men Scryfys
Nine Maidens
Tredinneck
Castle an Dinas
Gulval Downs
Boscaswell
Bojewyan
Portheras
Levant Mine
Chun Hill
Ding Dong
Ninnes
Chysauster
Newmill
Lanyon
Lanyon Quoit
Pendeen
Botallack Hd
Trewellard
Gt Bosullow
West Lanyon Quoit
Boswarthan
Noongallas
Badger's Cross
Botallack Mine
Carnyorth
Carn Bean
Boswens
Boswarva Carn
Madron Well
Trevaylor
Kenegie
Botallack
Carn Kenidjack
Boswarva
Trevaylor Stream
Kenidjack Cas.
Inn
Kenidjack
Porthledden
Boscean
Tregeseal
Tregerras
Madron
Gulval
Cape Cornwall
Inn
Newbridge
Poltair
Trengwainton Ho.
Hea Moor
Castle
Priest's Cove
Carn Gloose
Bellace Mine
St JUST
Balleswidden Mine
Larrigan R.
Trereife
Rosehill
PENZANCE
Nanven
The Brisons
Botrea
Tremethick Cross
Castle Horneck
Light Ho.
Bathing Pool
Bossavern
Bosworlas
Dowran
Golf Co.
Sellan
Gribba Pt.
Kelynack
Trewidden
Stable Hobba
Polpry Cove
Grumbla
The Beacon
Sancreed
Nancothan
Boscregan
Bartinney Downs
Bartine Cas.
Caer Bran
Buryas Br.
Tredavoe
Newlyn
Gwavas Lake
Nanquidno
Trevegean Downs
Tredinney
Drift
Tregonebris
Chyenhal
Carn Base
Aire Pt.
Carn Brea
Brea
Catchall
Quarry
Chydone
Paul Hill
Paul
Buoy
Low Lee
Whitesand Bay
Trevedra
Crows an wra
Leah
Boscawen
Nine Maidens
Kerris
Penlee Pt.
Escalls
Treave
Boscarn
Toldevas
Sheffield
L.B.Sta.
Mousehole
Cowloe
The Tribbens
Trevorian
Trevider
St Clement's Isle
Ship Inn
Irish Lady
Sennen Cove
Gamper B.
Table Men
Mayon
Mayon Cas.
Dr Syntax's Hd
Peal
Trevescan
Cliffs (N.T.)
Hotel
Penrose
St Buryan
Fowgow
Trewoofe
Castallack
Pt Spaniard
Sennen
Alsia
LANDS END
Boskennal
Boleigh
The Piper
Lamorna Valley
Kemyell
Trevescan
Skewjack
Trengothal
Armed Knight
Trevilley
Cross
Merry Maidens
Kemyell Cliff
Enys Dodman
Sparnon
Pardenack Pt
Polgigga
Tresidder
Boskenna
Boscowen Rôs
Lamorna Cove
Carn Boel
Trethewey
Trevedran
Tregiffian
Bosistow
Vineries
Rafra
Nanjizal B.
Gazell
Carn Les Boel
Logan Rock
Penberth
Treen
Pendower Cove
Porthcurno
Boscawen Pt.
Merthen Pt
Carn Barra
Roskestal
Porthguarnon
Penberth Cove
Folly Cove
Cribba Hd
St Levan
Treen Cliff
Treryn Dinas
Porth Loe
Carn Guthensbras
Porthcurno
Logan Rock
Chair Ladder
Gwennap Head
Porth Chapel
Wireless Sta.
Tol-Pedn Penwith
Porthgwarra
Pollostoc Zawn

a further thirty-five. The *City of Westminster* became a total wreck.

On March 20th 1926, the schooner *Ada*, of Barrow, with coal from Barry for Truro, struck some rocks near Cape Cornwall in rough ground sea, but refloated on the tide. A lifeboatman helped to pilot her to clear water, and the lifeboat also retrieved one of the *Ada's* crew in a small boat being carried away by wind and current. The schooner with six men on board eventually reached safety.

Between 1927-9 the Sennen station was entirely reconstructed to improve the launching arrangements, this work costing £11,000 to complete. A long launching slip was provided and a shorter hauling-up slip with turntable at its head for transferring the boat from one to the other. This represented a great improvement; but even today the boat cannot be launched for an hour and a half each side of low water, whilst re-housing is also sometimes impossible during certain states of tide or weather, the boat then having to make for Newlyn or St. Ives.

The Newbons launched at 9 p.m. on June 26th 1932, when the s.s. *Isadora*, of Cardiff, homeward bound in ballast, went ashore at Pendeen in fine weather. She was recalled when off Cape Cornwall, the steamer having by then refloated and gone on her way. Two years later, on July 14th the fishing ketch *Replete*, of Brixham, whilst trawling at night off the Wolf, fouled a submerged wreck, and soon after a fire broke out behind the boiler used for working the trawl-winch. Failing to extinguish the flames, the crew took to their small boat, and were picked up by another Brixham fishing vessel, the *Radiance*. The flames were seen from the shore, and the lifeboat launched at 12.15 a.m. on the 15th. She found the *Replete* ablaze from stem to stern, and, falling in with the *Radiance*, transferred the ketch's crew, standing by the burning vessel until she sank at 4.30 a.m.

During the afternoon of February 16th 1937, Coxswain Thomas Pender was informed by the Coastguard that a steamer with her engines broken down required help about a mile north of the Longships. A strong N.W. gale gusting to 90 m.p.h. was blowing with a very rough sea. The lifeboat launched at 4.20 p.m. and found the Danish steamer *Swanhild*, of Elsinore, in ballast, at anchor with a small steamer standing by. The lifeboat also stood by until the vessel's engines had been repaired, enabling her to go on her way, and then, as conditions were too bad to permit rehousing, she made for Penzance, arriving there at 9 p.m. She returned to her station two days later.

The schooner *Bretonne*, of Treguier, with coal from Cardiff for Brest, whilst sheltering in Whitesand Bay from a S.E. gale on December 18th

1938, parted one cable and dragged the other, being also in a leaky condition. About 8.5 p.m. the lifeboat launched in response to the schooner's flares, and threw a heaving line to her, by which means the crew of five were saved. She arrived back at 9.45 p.m., but being low tide they had to wait in bitterly cold weather until she could be rehoused at 11.30. By morning the schooner had disappeared, having apparently foundered.

This station rendered valuable assistance during the Second World War, both to shipping and air casualties. Following a naval and air battle ten miles off the Wolf Rock, on November 25th 1940, the Sennen, Penlee and Lizard boats made a search for survivors, but found nothing except a large patch of oil. On February 2nd 1941 the lifeboat launched at 6 p.m. in a strong N.E. gale and very rough sea to the s.s. *Heire*, of Oslo, which had lost her propeller three miles W.N.W. of the Brisons. She was waiting for a tug, and did not need the lifeboat's help, which accordingly returned to station, the crew standing by. Three hours later the steamer fired a red rocket, and it was thought she was ashore on the Shark's Fin, near the Longships. The weather had by then worsened, and the lifeboat could not be re-launched, but the *W. & S.* put out from Penlee at midnight and found the *Heire* in a very dangerous position still waiting for a tug. She stood by until the tug arrived nine hours later, and then returned to her station at noon on the 3rd.

Red flares were reported off Cape Cornwall on April 14th 1941, and the lifeboat put off, but found nothing. It later transpired that the flares were Holmes lights of lifebuoys of the Belgian steamer *Arbel*, of Antwerp, which had been blown off her when she was bombed and sunk. Seventeen survivors of her crew of twenty came ashore at St. Ives. The auxiliary cruiser *Registan* was bombed and set on fire by four enemy planes at about 10.45 p.m. on May 27th six miles N.W. of Sennen. The lifeboat was then undergoing an overhaul, but Second Coxswain Edward Nicholas and four other men put out in the motor fishing boat *Ruby* at 11 p.m., the weather being fine at the time. Close to the burning steamer they rescued four men from a raft, one badly injured. Their morse lamp attracted an enemy plane, however, which flew over the motor boat and machine-gunned her crew, but without doing them any damage, and the rescued men were landed at Sennen at 3.15 a.m.

The Sennen boat made a search during the night of September 12-13th 1942 when an aeroplane crashed about four miles N.W. of

Cape Cornwall, but found only fragments of the plane and burning oil. Another aeroplane was reported down 200 yards off Pendeen lighthouse at 2.23 p.m. on October 8th 1942, and two men from her drifting N.E. in a squally N.W. wind and rough sea. The lifeboat was launched eleven minutes later and a Lysander aeroplane guided her to where the two airmen in "Mae West" jackets were floating unconscious. The lifeboat took them on board, but efforts at resuscitation proved unavailing. They also picked up a rubber dinghy dropped from the Lysander. She returned to Sennen at 5 p.m. but could not land the bodies until 6.18 owing to the state of tide. The St. Ives lifeboat also launched to this casualty, but was recalled after being three hours at sea.

On December 24th 1942 a Whitley bomber crashed in the area, four of its crew being rescued by a patrol trawler and the rest drowned. A Spitfire was reported down on May 1st 1943, but nothing could be found; whilst the lifeboat made another vain search for a small fishing boat with crew of two missing on June 27th 1944. Three days later, at 8.18 p.m. Longships lighthouse reported a boat adrift about half a mile N.W. of that position as a possible danger to navigation. The lifeboat went out in a squally N.W. wind and found the U.S. Army motor launch MT.392 near the Brisons, apparently abandoned in a hurry with personal effects still on board. She towed the craft back to Sennen, arriving at 11.15 p.m.

At 3.30 p.m. on January 21st 1945, *The Newbons* launched to the assistance of the torpedoed "Liberty" steamer *George Hawley*[1] four miles S. by W. of the Longships. She reached the vessel at 4.40, and found that all her crew except five had already been taken off or had got away. As everything was covered in oil, these five entered their own boat and the lifeboat towed them to a tug, which had now attached a rope to the *George Hawley*. The tug eventually brought the vessel to Falmouth, only two lives being lost during this incident. Penlee lifeboat also launched that afternoon, but arrived too late to help.

An explosion was heard at 3.40 p.m. on March 22nd 1945, and it was seen that a vessel had been torpedoed about seven miles N.W. of Sennen. *The Newbons* launched with a moderate E.S.E. wind but calm sea, and on reaching the scene was signalled by an escort vessel to come alongside her. She had forty-nine of the crew of the torpedoed ship, the s.s. *Empire Kingsley*, of Greenock, on board, and these were transferred to the lifeboat and landed, including four injured men on stretchers.

The lifeboat launched at 7.45 a.m. on March 29th 1945 to frigate

1. Possibly the *George Handley*, of Savannah, Ga.

K.458 of the Royal Canadian Navy then four miles N.N.W. of Pen-men-dhu, having been torpedoed and her stern nearly blown off. She found the damaged vessel at 8.25 and on going alongside, was asked to search in the frigate's wake for two missing men. She found one of these, and returned and stood by until another vessel took the casualty in tow. She accompanied them for some way, but as a large tug was coming to take over the tow and the Penlee lifeboat *W. & S.* had arrived, she returned to station. Difficulties were encountered when the tug had towed the frigate some distance, so after the latter had anchored, 57 of her crew were taken off by the *W. & S.* and eventually landed at Newlyn. The K.458 eventually reached Falmouth, but was a constructive total loss, and saw no further service before being broken up in December 1945.

A new 41 ft. motor lifeboat of the Watson type—the first of this class to have a cabin—arrived at Sennen on July 26th 1948, and is still rendering excellent service there. Named *Susan Ashley*, she was provided from the legacy of Charles Carr Ashley Esq., of Mentone. Two 35 h.p. engines give her a speed of eight knots, and wireless and a loud hailer are included in her equipment. The inaugural ceremony for this boat had been fixed for September 4th, but just before 8 a.m. the previous day the *Susan Ashley* launched to assist a trawler with engine trouble in a N.W. gale. The trawler effected repairs and went on her way before the lifeboat could reach her, and, the weather being too bad for rehousing, the *Susan Ashley* made for Newlyn, where she remained till the 5th. As a result, she was not present for her inauguration, which went forward as planned, except for the naming ceremony which then took place on October 2nd, being performed by Lady Burnett.

When the forepart of the steamer *Empire Flamingo* was being towed from Arromanches to Newport for breaking up on October 26th 1948, she began to sink three miles south of the Longships, and one of the two tugs accompanying her requested the lifeboat to take off the four men on board. The *Susan Ashley* launched at 8.33 in a moderate north breeze with heavy ground swell and rescued the four men, landing them at Newlyn. On the way, a wireless message was received saying the hulk had foundered. The *Empire Flamingo*, classed as a Special Service Vessel, had been sunk as a blockship in February 1944 on one of the Normandy beaches. She was an old American cargo liner of 5,200 tons, originally named *Jolee*.

A most dramatic shipwreck and rescue occurred on November 3rd 1962 when the trawler *Jeanne Gougy* of Dieppe, bound for the south

Irish fishing grounds, went ashore during the early morning on the north side of the Land's End headland. The Sennen Coxswain having been informed by the Coastguard of the casualty at 5.21 a.m., the reserve lifeboat on temporary duty at the station was launched and reached the scene in an hour. By a parachute flare, they saw the trawler lying on her side on rocks at the foot of the cliff. An exceptionally heavy ground swell prevailed, the aftermath of a recent storm, and it was impossible to take the lifeboat closer in than a hundred yards. An L.S.A. team at the cliff top had fired several lines over, but the trawler's crew could not secure them as their craft was completely submerged by the swell, several men having been washed out of her wheelhouse. At 8.15 a helicopter from Chivenor arrived, and with the lifeboat carried out a search for these. The lifeboat found two, and the helicopter one, but all were dead, and at 9 a.m. the helicopter left for Penzance to land a body and to refuel at Culdrose.

As there then appeared to be no one left alive on the *Jeanne Gougy*, the lifeboat made for Newlyn to land the bodies, it being impossible to return to Sennen. At noon, however, a woman watching from the cliff top saw a man's hand waving inside the wheelhouse and heard him calling. The coastguards fired a line over the trawler, and a man, clinging to the edge of the wheelhouse doorway which then faced the sky, as the vessel was completely on her side, struggled to grasp it, but was prevented by heavy waves. Eventually he secured the line, and was hauled to safety in the breeches buoy, three others being afterwards rescued by the same means. The helicopter, on being recalled, hovered over the ship, and lowered a man who saved two more seamen. These six had survived by breathing air trapped in pockets in the wheelhouse and forecastle. On learning of these developments, the Penlee lifeboat *Solomon Browne* launched at 12.45 and arrived at 2, whilst the Sennen boat also returned to the scene at 3.45. With the helicopter, they again searched the area, but without result. It was learned that the trawler carried a crew of 18, twelve of whom lost their lives, including the skipper. Sergeant E. C. Smith, of the R.A.F., who was lowered to the *Jeanne Gougy* to save two injured men, received the George Medal and also the Silver Medal of the Société Nationale des Hospitaliers Sauveteurs Bretons. The stirring events connected with this shipwreck, which received extensive press and television coverage, provided an excellent illustration for the public of the manner of working of the three principal types of sea rescue services in this country and of the co-operation existing between them.

The *Susan Ashley* carried out a most daring rescue on March 24th 1964, when the trawler *Victoire Roger*, of Ostend, ran ashore under the precipitous cliffs in lonely Gamper Cove, near Land's End, during thick fog and darkness. The crew were working on deck preparing the nets when she struck at about 4 a.m., and they at once put out a distress call, showed red lights and burned blankets and beds to draw attention to their plight. An auxiliary watcher at Sennen saw their signals, and through the Coastguard Station at St. Just directed the Sennen lifeboat straight to the wreck. Coxswain Henry Nicholas found *Victoire Roger* in a most difficult position within a deep cleft. Fortunately the mist had cleared when they arrived, but there was a nasty sea, whilst the whole operation had to be carried out in darkness, the lifeboatmen having only their own deck lights and the fire on the trawler to work by. The Coxswain first considered dropping an anchor and firing a line on board, but seeing the men aft, decided to make a quick run in and snatch some off. They had very little room in which to manoeuvre, being up against the side of the trawler, and could almost touch the cliff with a boathook. They succeeded in pulling off four men as they went alongside, but in coming astern the sea went over the lifeboat's stern. The lifeboat crew then learned that a fifth man—the skipper—was still on board, with a broken arm, and they made a second run in to get him. The *Susan Ashley* bumped on the bottom two or three times when carrying out this operation, but sustained no damage. The rescued men were then taken to Newlyn harbour and safely landed at 6.15 a.m. Penlee lifeboat also launched in response to the trawler's radio distress call, and made an unsuccessful search for her in the Porthcurno area. The *Victoire Roger* went ashore near the spot where the *Jeanne Gougy* had been wrecked in 1962.

BOAT RECORD, SENNEN COVE

Years on Station	Length, Breadth, Depth	Type, Oars, Crew	Weight, Cost, O. No.	Built, Year, Builder	Boat's Name, Donor, Authority
1853- 1864	25′ 8″ 6′ 10″ 3′ 5″	Peake 6 9	1t8 £125	1853 Forrestt, Limehouse	? National Shipwreck [Institution do.
1864- 1880	33′ 8′ 3′ 10″	SR 10	 £250	1864 Forrestt, Limehouse	*Cousins William and Mary Ann of Bideford* Mrs. M. A. Davis, Bideford R.N.L.I.

1880-	34′	SR		1880[1]	*Denzil and Maria Onslow*
1893	8′ 3″	10	£363	Woolfe,	Miss Maria Onslow,
			182	Shadwell	R.N.L.I. [Faygate, Sussex
1893-	35′	SR	3t17	1893	*Ann Newbon*
1922	8′ 3″	10	£498	Woolfe,	Legacy Mr. R. A. Newbon,
			357	Shadwell	R.N.L.I. [Islington
1922-	40′	SR(M)	11t16	1922	*The Newbons*[2]
1948	10′ 6″	—	£8622	White & Co.	Legacy Mr. R. A. Newbon,
		9	674	E. Cowes	R.N.L.I. [Islington
1948-	41′	WC(M)	14t16	1948	*Susan Ashley*
	11′ 8″	—	£13357	Groves & G.,	Legacy Charles Carr Ashley,
		8	856	E. Cowes	R.N.L.I. [Mentone

1 Altered and improved 1888.
2 Replacing four pulling and sailing lifeboats named after Ann, Betsey, Lucy and Nancy Newbon.

[This station was under the management of Penzance until mid-1914.]

SERVICE RECORD, SENNEN COVE

First Lifeboat				
1856	May	6-7	Barque *Charles Adolphe*, of La Rochelle, assisted to save vessel	
Cousins William and Mary Ann of Bideford Lifeboat				
1865	Oct.	13	Longships lighthouse, landed a keeper seriously ill; saved	1
1868	Oct.	23	Government lighter *Devon*, saved	1
Denzil and Maria Onslow Lifeboat				
1883	Jan.	8	Cutter *Spring*, of Guernsey, saved vessel and	3
1889	Oct.	15	s.s. *Malta*, of Glasgow, rendered assistance and saved	7
Ann Newbon Lifeboat				
1894	Dec.	24	H.M.S. *Lynx*, rendered assistance	
1895	Oct.	17	s.s. *Harberton*, of London, assisted to save vessel	
1898	Nov.	10	s.s. *Blue Jacket*, of Cardiff, saved	22
1901	Oct.	21	Two fishing boats of Sennen Cove, landed 5	
	Nov.	18	Schooner *Mary James*, of Penzance, saved	6
1902	May	27	H.M.S. *Recruit*, stood by	
1903	Feb.	4	Boat of s.s. *Benwick*, of Newcastle, saved	5
1908	Dec.	29	Ship *Fairport*, of Liverpool, assisted to save vessel and	20
1910	Mar.	13	Trawler *Harry*, of Brixham, saved trawler's boat and	4
1912	Feb.	29	s.s. *Northlands*, of Cardiff, stood by	
	Mar.	14	Trawler *Condor*, of Brixham, stood by	
1913	Apr.	4	Ketch *Woolwich Infant*, of Falmouth, stood by	
	Aug.	14	s.s. *J. Duncan*, of Cardiff, landed 2 and saved	12
1917	Feb.	20	H.M. Seaplane, saved	1
	Apr.	20	s.s. *Polyktor*, of Ithaca, saved	28
	Sept.	10	s.s. *Ioanna*, of London, landed 3	
1918	Feb.	7	s.s. *Beaumaris*, of London, stood by, rendered assistance and saved	18

1919	Mar.	17	s.s. *Falmouth Castle*, of Falmouth, landed 7	
	Apr.	29	Boat of s.s. *Frisia*, of Rotterdam, saved	14
	Nov.	30	H.M. Motor Launch 378, saved	8
1920	Sept.	22	Motor Fishing Boat *Our Boys*, of Porthleven, saved	5
1921	Jan.	22	s.s. *Haliartus*, of Liverpool, assisted to save vessel	
	Aug.	16	Barge *Strumble*, of London, saved vessel	

The Newbons Lifeboat

1923	Sept.	29	s.s. *Gutfeld*, of Hamburg, rendered assistance	
	Oct.	8	s.s. *City of Westminster*, of Liverpool, saved	13
1926	Mar.	20	Schooner *Ada*, of Barrow, assisted to save vessel and	6
	Apr.	20	s.s. *Deansway*, of Cardiff, stood by	
1931	Aug.	29	A small boat of Priest's Cove, saved boat and	3
1934	July	15	Fishing ketch *Replete*, of Brixham, landed 4	
1936	Feb.	10	Boat of ketch *Albatros*, of Brest, saved a dog and	4
	Dec.	21	s.s. *Mina*, of Parnu, rendered assistance and stood by	
1937	Feb.	16	s.s. *Swanhild*, of Elsinore, stood by	
1938	Dec.	18	Schooner *Bretonne*, of Treguier, saved	5
1942	Sept.	12	Aeroplane in sea, salved wreckage	
	Oct.	8	Aeroplane, picked up two bodies and salved rubber dinghy	
1944	June	30	U.S. Army Motor Launch MT.392, saved launch	
1945	Jan.	21	s.s. *George Hawley*, of Savannah, Ga., saved	5
	Feb.	24	Unknown vessel torpedoed, wreckage found	
	Mar.	22	s.s. *Empire Kingsley*, of Greenock, landed 49	
		29	H.M. Frigate *Teme*, of the Royal Canadian Navy, rendered assistance and stood by	

Susan Ashley Lifeboat

1948	Oct.	11	s.s. *Woodlark*, of London, gave help and transferred one survivor of the fishing boat *Saphir*, of Camaret, to another craft	
		26	Ex-War Dept. hulk *Empire Flamingo*, saved	4
1952	Jan.	6	Took doctors and a nurse to Scilly, thereby saving	1
	July	20	Yacht *Morena*, of London, rendered assistance	
1953	Apr.	18	Yacht *Larry*, of Southampton, saved yacht and	3
1956	July	30	Yacht *Westo II*, of Southampton, saved yacht	
1961	June	28	French trawler *Enfant des Houles*, rendered assistance	
1962	May	9	Man trapped on cliff, landed a body	
	July	9	Cabin cruiser *Eldora*, towed in cruiser	
		28	Swimmers on rocks, saved	2
	Aug.	4	Motor Tug *Sally*, of Rochester, rendered assistance	
		25	Girl on rocks, landed a body	

Edmund and Mary Robinson (Reserve) Lifeboat

1962	Nov.	3	Trawler *Jeanne Gougy*, of Dieppe, landed two bodies	

Susan Ashley Lifeboat

1963	Sept.	13	m.v. *Alacrity*, of London, gave help and stood by	
1964	Mar.	24	Trawler *Victoire Roger*, of Ostend, saved	5

3

ISLES OF SCILLY

LIKE THE mainland of Cornwall, the Isles of Scilly have acquired the two strangely opposing reputations of a holiday paradise, and a place notorious for shipwrecks. And of course both are true. No explanation is needed for the former, but for the technically minded one must explain that the latter have, in the vast majority of cases, been caused by a slight, but constant, northward current from Biscay. This, through the ages, has sent innumerable craft off course among the islands as they pass on their lawful occasions. Even today when navigational aids of extreme complication can lessen the perils of the sea, every so often a disaster jolts us into realising that the elements can still treat us with impunity, although, of course, such dangers are not confined to this fascinating corner of the kingdom.

In the well known figure-head collection at the 'Valhalla' in the grounds of Tresco Abbey, the Scillies possess a unique reminder of bygone wrecks. Founded by the then Lord Proprietor, Augustus Smith, in the middle of the last century, there are forty or more figure-heads, fiddleheads, and other relics, recently painstakingly restored to their original form and colours. The fixed, admonitory stares of king and queen, maiden, friar and soldier, and a host of others, seem to bid us remember old sea battles where the prizes were lives snatched from the destructive sea.

As far as writing goes, some of the famous disasters of the Scillies have been described almost too often, but nevertheless, shipwrecks are an essential part of our sea story, and one hopes that the chronicling commenced by Miss Charlotte Dorrien Smith, and the further researches of many, such as Miss Juliet du Boulay and Richard Gillis, can be extended to a complete and authoritative study.

Miss Dorrien Smith has pointed out Troutbeck's statement that the gentlemen of Scilly sent a vessel to the aid of casualties as early as 1790, he quoting an instance when a Dutch ship was helped. It would be interesting to know more of this craft, although it is fairly certain to have been a gig used as occasion demanded for boarding pilots and other 'hobbling' work. As is well known, the pilots and their assistants carried out many a fine rescue in their gigs, which they handled with consummate skill and daring. There were excellent grounds for the tribute paid to them, perhaps unconsciously, in *The Pilot's Handbook for the English Channel* of 1863. The "Scilly Islands possess several harbours . . . but none of them should be taken by a stranger without a pilot, whose attendance may be depended on, even in the worst weather, as soon as the pilot signal is made".

At various times the pilots have themselves lost their lives in attempting to rescue wrecked crews, or in boarding vessels seeking shelter. An early instance was on January 27th 1815, when the outward bound West-Indiaman *Queen Charlotte* of Glasgow came ashore in a strong gale accompanied by heavy snow falls. She broke up almost immediately and three passengers and one seaman were lost. Fourteen others, lashed to a mast, were thrown on to a rock to which they clung through two bitter nights, ill clad and without food. To quote the typically fulsome contemporary press.—"On the 28th the crews of numerous boats from the islands attempted to rescue the unfortunate men, but so resistless was the force of the storm that after many ineffectual endeavours they were compelled to return, and the distressed mariners to pass another dreadful night in that exposed situation, under the most severe privation. With the dawn of the Sabbath the most resolute exertions were made. The crew of a stout boat, after braving every danger, succeeded in reaching the perilous place, and in effecting the preservation of five of the almost famished men". On a second attempt, "having rescued a poor negro, and being in the act of securing several others, a heavy wave carried away two of the islanders. The loss of their brave associates did not check for a moment the generous spirit of the natives. They renewed their humane exertions, and by indefatigable perseverance, happily succeeded with the aid of providence, in saving fourteen lives". The lost pilots were Charles Jackson and James Tregarthen, the latter having only recently returned home after nine weary years as a prisoner of war with the French. Happily a subscription list was opened for the widows and children with £100 from Lloyd's, and 50 guineas from the Duke of Leeds, then Governor and Lord Proprietor of the Islands.

Picking two other early gig rescues at random:—In February 1830, the *Borodino*, from Sierra Leone, called in the Roads for orders and was directed to Milford for discharging. As she got under weigh again she made too much leeway and was driven on the rocks at Carn Morval. Her complement of 21, including pilots for Scilly and Milford, were

The Italian steamer Aida Lauro *(4538 tons), her back broken in two places, near Botallack Head, July 1st 1937*

The s.s. Malta *(2244 tons) which drove ashore in fog, south of Botallack Head, St Just, October 15th 1889. No lives were lost but the vessel was a total loss (Photo: Gibson)*

The collier Datetree, *wrecked on The Brisons, June 25th 1914*

H.M. Submarine L.1 *ashore south of Cape Cornwall. The Brisons are visible off-shore*

The s.s. Ixia, *of North Shields, off the cliffs below St Just, July 5th 1929 (Photos: Gibson)*

The Cardiff steamer Blue Jacket *(2090 tons) unaccountably wrecked on a clear night on the Longships, November 10th 1898. Her crew of 22 were saved by the Sennen Cove lifeboat (Photo: Gibson)*

Sennen Cove lifeboat The Newbons *returning from a mission in the 1930's. Note the launching slip on the left and re-housing slip on the right. Within the house, the boat is re-aligned on a turntable for re-launching*

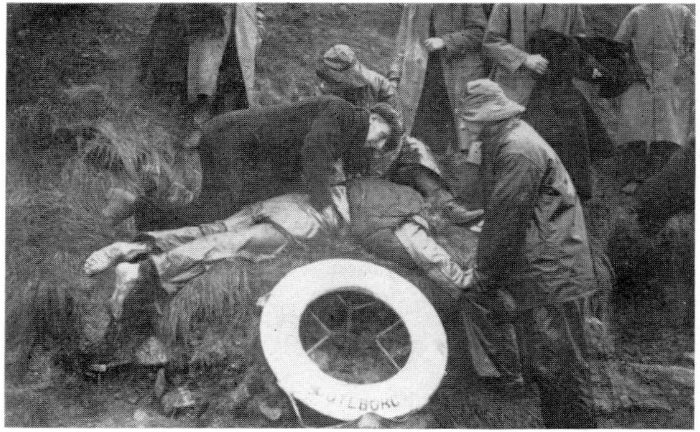

Scenes at and after the wreck of the steel barque Trifolium, *of Goteborg, at Whitesand Bay (Sennen) March 15th 1914. Six of her crew were saved by the Coastguard but five others were drowned. The mass of twisted metal (lower right) was all that remained of the vessel after the next tide (Photo: Gibson)*

saved by the prompt and daring efforts of the gigs *Champion*, *Dove* and *Blucher*. Again, in 1838, the schooner *Victoria*, of Exeter, was wrecked in Crow Sound and the gigs *Bee*, *Bull* and *Juno*, with support from the pilot cutter *Active*, saved her crew of six. Of the men engaged in this rescue at least twelve were members of the Hicks family, one of several whose names appear time and again in the sea story of the Islands.

There is no doubt that before steam vessels became available for towage, the off-island gigs were the best means of lifesaving in so complex an area. With the difficulty of making one central position serve as a lifesaving station for the whole group, it is small wonder that the first lifeboats proved to be seldom utilized.

Unfortunately, of the first lifeboat sent out to St. Mary's in 1837 by the "National Shipwreck Institution", nothing is known, apart from the fact that the Inspecting Commander of the Coast Guard, Captain Charles Steel, R.N., had much to do with its introduction and the organisation of the station. With the pilots and their helpers preferring to put off in their own light boats, it usually fell to the coast guard to provide the greater part of the crew. This first lifeboat was short-lived, being replaced three years later by a boat moved from the Plymouth station. The second boat, however, was on station until 1855 and brief details of her appear in the Northumberland Report of 1851. She was of the type designed by Pellew Plenty of Newbury, Berkshire, the first "standard" boat adopted by the Institution, and had been built in 1828, was 26 ft. long, and pulled ten oars. She was then stated to be "in good repair" and to "pull fairly". Like her predecessor she was kept in a stone house fronting the Town Beach at Thorofare, built for the purpose in 1838, size 30 ft. by 11 ft.

Steel himself led the lifeboat crew on their only recorded service of this period. It was a tragic affair and they appear to have played but a minor role. Just before seven in the morning of January 4th 1841, the steam packet *Thames*, bound from Dublin for London, was seen to the west, apparently disabled, and lying at the mercy of a heavy westerly gale which was relentlessly driving her into a position of extreme danger. It later transpired that there had been some confusion over lights fitfully seen through the snow squalls, and that seas had found their way below to put out the boiler fires. Thus helpless, it was clear she must foul some part of that reef which stands like a wall at the south-west of the Islands—the Western Rocks. Soon she struck Jacky's Rock and her crew then fired blue lights to summon help. Preparations were at once made at St. Agnes and St. Mary's, but what actually happened is obscured by differences in various accounts; those of the Reverend George Woodley (as published later in pamphlet form), the Annual Report of the Life-boat Institution, and two reports in the *Penzance Gazette.* It appears that the St. Agnes gig *Thomas* was first launched, followed by the *Bee* and *Briton*, and later, when the tide floated her, by the pilot cutter *Active.* At St. Mary's Captain Steel called for volunteers, but, possibly because the life-boat was largely untried, some encouragement was needed. At first only four men came forward—William Rowe and Patrick O'Neill, coast guards; Barnard Hicks, seaman; and James Hyde, labourer. However, a full crew was mustered after a slight delay and soon, like the gigs, they were struggling at the oars against mountainous seas and through squalls of hail and sleet. The *Thomas* reached the scene first and, with what must have been superhuman efforts, they got close enough to catch a line by which means they hauled themselves under the steamer's weather quarter. Captain James Grey, in the best tradition, sent down the women first. Cecilia Morris was dragged from her father's agonised grasp and passed down to the boat. Then a sea filled the boat and the next two, who were stewardesses named Mary Mylor (or Naylor), and Mary Gregory, had to be dragged through the sea. But then disaster came. A sudden squall whipped up the waves, and with the boat plunging and tossing uncontrollably it became impossible to maintain contact. They had to pull back and join the other boats which were getting what shelter they could under the lee of Gorregan. The women were soaked through and numbed. To give them some small protection they were transferred to a boat which had a small cuddy in her bows, probably the *Active.* Soon afterwards, it being obvious they would die of exposure unless given attention, they were taken back to St. Agnes, landing at 3 p.m. The other boats continued to hover near the wreck, waiting to seize any chance of a lull during which they could close in for a rescue, but they were frustrated. On the wreck, giving up hope, some army recruits, 20 or so in number, launched the two ship's boats, but every soul perished. The sailors lashed together rafts and as the main mast of the *Thames* broke adrift, tearing up the decks, and finishing the work of the waves in a few minutes, they floated off, only to be upset and dashed ashore on Rosevear. It is possible several were alive when they reached this small island, but only one survived the night. This man, seaman Edward Kerrom (or Kearson, or Kearon), managed to gain a precarious foothold and, evidently a man of resource, is said to have spent the night inside a cask stuffed with grass. It was dark early, of course, and the waiting Islanders knew nobody could have survived on the pitiful remnants of wreck, but they resolved to stay the night so that they could search the rocks at daylight. So it came about that one of the boats found Kerrom, and from him learnt that as far as Rosevear was concerned there were no other survivors but several bodies. The lifeboat then landed a couple of men and, from the rock and sea, eight bodies were collected to be brought back to St. Mary's for burial.

The wreck of the *Thames* was indeed a terrible affair. She is said to have had a crew of 26, and 35 passengers, although accounts differ. This would indicate some 57 lives lost. One feels that every possible effort was made by the Islanders in the face of impossible conditions. Whilst it is purely academic to question which boat did what, one hopes that due justice has been done to all concerned. In fact the Institution's Gold Medal was awarded to Steel, its Silver Medal to each of the original four volunteers in the lifeboat, and cash rewards to the others in the lifeboat and the crews of the three gigs. Doubtless collections were made locally as well.

Continuing the story of the lifeboat:—between the *Thames* rescue and 1855, in which year the station was disbanded, she made no rescues. She was, to the end, described as being "in fair repair" and was managed latterly by Thomas Johns Buxton, one of the principal local ship agents. A dozen or so wrecks are recorded in this period, including several where disaster was sudden and complete before any help could have been afforded, and others where vessels, already abandoned by their crews, were driven among the islands.

The station was re-established after a gap of almost twenty years. At a committee meeting of the R.N.L.I. on March 5th 1874, it was "decided to form a life-boat station at St. Mary's." The contemporary official journal explained—"For many years it had been in contemplation to station a life-boat at Scilly, but wrecks not being very frequent in the neighbourhood and local difficulties arising, the question had been postponed from time to time". And in another issue: "It had been considered by persons there that, as the majority of wrecks occurred in foggy weather with light winds, aid could more rapidly be given by the fast-pulling pilot gigs of the boatmen".

There had, in fact, been several wrecks in the Islands, the most serious being those of the *Minnehaha* and *Delaware*. The former, a four-masted barque of Londonderry was wrecked in fog on Peninnis Head in 1871, while bound for Dublin from Falmouth where she had called for orders. Ten, including the Captain, were drowned, and another ten were able to clamber ashore at low tide after a nerve-racking night on the forepart, which was held by the rocks.

The steamship *Delaware*, of Liverpool, with a crew of 44, was wrecked on Mincarlo in December of the same year while outward bound for Calcutta. She had engine trouble, and in spite of frantic efforts to keep clear of the Islands, was driven into their midst by an exceptionally heavy gale. After striking, she drove over the reef. Then a heavy sea carried away her bridge and caused her cargo to shift. Another found its way below, and she foundered in deeper water near Samson—all in a matter of minutes. The first and third mates were washed to White Island on a fragment of ship's boat and thrown ashore badly injured. Three others were seen clinging to wreckage in the sea. Without delay ten Bryher men, with tremendous perseverance, dragged their six-oared gig *Albion* across to the south bay, launched her, landed on Samson, dragged her across the neck of the island, and then relaunched her to pull to White Island. All this was done in the face of terrible weather conditions, and by the time they arrived the two men on the rock were the only survivors. These they got back to Bryher in another boat, leaving the *Albion* on the weather side of Samson until the next day. These were two disastrous wrecks, relieved only by the bravery of the Bryher men, but in fairness it is doubtful if a lifeboat could have averted loss of life in either case.

The 1874 lifeboat was a great advance on earlier models. She was a 37 ft. self-righter, designed for sailing, but pulling twelve oars when necessary. She was named *Henry Dundas*, being built from the legacy of Mrs. Dundas Drummond, and after being towed from Penzance was ceremonially launched on 1st August. A house was built for her at Porth Cressa from which she could be taken on her carriage for launching either into the nearby bay, or across the town into the harbour, according to the position of the casualty.

Rather less than a year later she was called to a disastrous wreck on the Retarriers. The trans-Atlantic liner *Schiller*, of the Adler Line, Hamburg, on her homeward trip from New York with 384 persons on board, ran into dense fog when approaching the Scillies and nobody realised she had passed inside the Bishop Rock. She drove on the reef when travelling at half speed and was held firmly by the bows while the stern sank rapidly. Only one of her guns was heard at St. Mary's and, because it was the usual practice, albeit a foolish one, for liners to fire a gun on first sighting land, no notice was taken. Most of the *Schiller*'s boats were carried away by the waves before they could be launched, and only two of them survived the night. On board, the angle of the decks, the darkness, and the falling of the funnel soon after she struck, caused panic, and the Captain had to fire his pistol to restore order. Having no further means of signalling they were not seen until dawn, and then two gigs promptly put off from St. Agnes. The seas were still too confused for the gigs to go alongside and save the few survivors clinging to the fore and main masts, but one, the *O. and M.*, picked up five from the water and returned to call the lifeboat. The *Henry Dundas* was towed out by the steam packet *Lady of the Isles*, but by the time she arrived the masts had fallen and all she could do was find some bodies and 23 bags of mails. The two ship's boats that survived the night got to Tresco in the morning without local help, thanks to expert handling by the officers in charge. Once again, the rescue boats had done all that could be done in the circumstances, and fortunately one benefit resulted for the practice of liners firing a gun on approaching land was discontinued by mutual consent. The number of survivors of this disaster is not clear, having been variously given as 43, 41 and 34.

The first successful service of the *Henry Dundas* took place on October 28th 1880, when the brig *Messenger*, of Salcombe, bound from Cardiff for Portsmouth with steam coal for the Navy, dragged her anchors in a very heavy S.S.W. gale and stranded on Skirt Island, Tresco. The rocket apparatus soon established communication, but the line fouled on some rocks and Mr. Dorrien Smith bravely pulled himself out to the rock, where he was able to clear the tangle. However, it so happened that this method was not used, as the lifeboat arrived to take off five men, afterwards standing by as the Captain and two men wished to remain on board. At daylight the brig was refloated and the crew put back.

Just over a year later, on November 27th 1881, there was a casualty which afterwards provided some exciting moments for the Islanders. The barque *Excelsior*, of Hamburg, from Rangoon with rice, called for discharging orders and was caught in the Roads by a rising westerly gale and heavy seas. About 3.30 in the afternoon she parted two cables, and being left riding to her sole spare anchor, signals of distress were made. The lifeboat went off, also two gigs, one each from Bryher and St. Mary's. The gigs rowed furiously through terrible weather with extra men at the oars, arriving on either side of the *Excelsior*, unknown to each other. The scene can well be imagined as they ran aft to be first to get the job. It is said that the Captain was very drunk, but in any case all three crews were engaged to board and assist saving the vessel.

They slipped the remaining anchor, hoisted a jib, and ran her over Crow Bar on to the sandy beach east of Cruther's Point, St. Martin's. The lifeboat then stood by through the night and eventually got back to station in the morning after sixteen hours on watch. During the following months the barque's cargo was taken out and she was temporarily patched. On January 22nd the steamer *Queen of the Bay* was taken alongside to give extra pumping power, and the *Lady of the Isles* took her in tow for St. Mary's harbour for more extensive repairs. Unfortunately she touched bottom in crossing Crow Bar, causing her to fall over on the *Queen of the Bay*, snapping her mainmast like a twig. With difficulty the packet was extricated, but the barque settled down on her beam ends, there being many anxious moments while the pumping gangs of Islanders, some fifty in number, were hurriedly taken off. The *Excelsior* had to be written off as a total loss.

The last service of the first *Henry Dundas* was in some respects her most successful. On the night of June 9th 1887, in dense fog, the steamer *Castleford*, of Liverpool, went ashore on Crebawethan, one of the notorious Western Rocks. She was bound from Montreal for London, and besides general cargo, had 450 cattle on board. Some of the crew left in their own boats and reached St. Agnes, whence word was telegraphed to St. Mary's and the lifeboat was launched at midnight. There was a heavy swell and the flowing tide to contend with, but the lifeboat ferried 25 men to a ship's boat which one of the lifeboatmen piloted to St. Mary's. She then herself took 25 men ashore, afterwards returning to stand by until daylight. Eventually a large number of the cattle were saved and put to pasture on Annet until they could be shipped away.

At this period the Institution was building some large lifeboats on the standard pattern, but heavier, and adapted for sailing rather longer distances than most normal station boats. It was decided to try one of these at St. Mary's, where she could be kept afloat in the harbour. This boat of $7\frac{1}{2}$ tons had two drop keels and three water ballast tanks, and at 42ft. long was one of the largest in the fleet at the time. She again bore the name *Henry Dundas*.

Within a few days of arrival she was called out in very heavy seas and thick weather to a vessel anchored close to the Western Rocks. This proved to be the brigantine *Antares*, of Nantes, bound for Llanelly with pit props and a crew of six. She was, in fact, in a desperate position, only a hundred yards from the dreaded Retarriers. Two gigs had attempted to approach to offer help, but had been defeated by the high seas. The lifeboat, however, managed to get alongside and put on board four men, one of whom was a pilot. While she made fast forward, all hands got the anchor up and the brigantine was towed and sailed well out of danger three miles beyond Bishop Rock.

Whether in fact the difficulties of manoeuvring a 42ft. boat close to rocks cancelled out any advantages in sailing qualities is not clear, but before many months were up the crew and the committee asked for

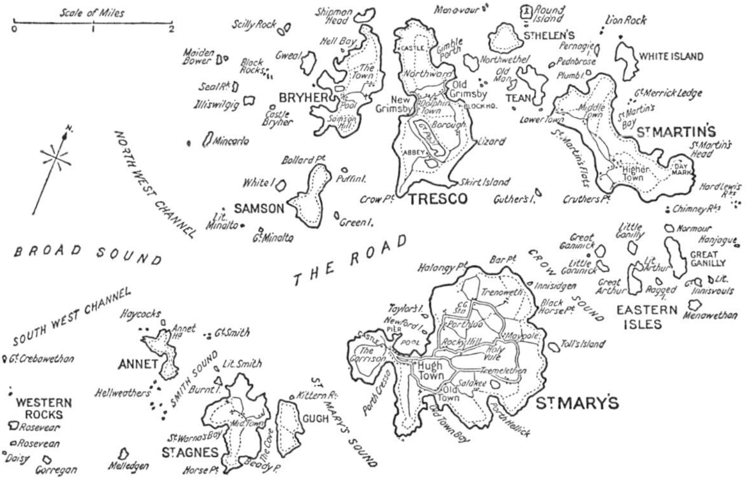

another boat of more normal size. The large one was sent to Beaumaris, in Anglesey, and a third *Henry Dundas*, 38ft. by 8ft., was sent in October. Possibly another reason for the smaller and obviously handier boat was the establishment of a station at Priglis Bay, St. Agnes, which had been opened in August with the 34ft., 10-oared boat, *James and Caroline*. This was the obvious answer for wrecks on the Western Rocks, which have claimed more victims than any other part of the Islands, but the local community was so small it was often difficult to obtain a full crew. However, it was the lack of horses for hauling the launching carriage which caused the most trouble, and by 1903 it was necessary to build a concrete slipway. Later extended, this became the longest lifeboat slipway in the kingdom, down which the lifeboat was launched on a bogie running on rails.

The first service of the St. Agnes lifeboat was during the tremendous blizzard which struck the West Country between March 9th and 12th 1891. At 4.30 p.m. on the 10th they sighted one of the ubiquitous little smacks which traded round the Cornish coast carrying culm for firing limestone, upon which the agricultural part of the community depended for soil dressing. This vessel, the *Porth*, of Padstow, was disabled by the loss of sails and quite at the mercy of the N.E. gale which raged, thick with snow. She struck before the lifeboat could reach her and one hand jumped overboard, swam to a rock, but was unfortunately washed off again and drowned. The smack drifted away again and stranded on Annet, her skipper and remaining hand landing in their own boat. When the lifeboat took them on board they were completely exhausted from their battering in the blizzard, and their subsequent efforts to get to the islet in their boat.

On April 4th 1893, the St. Mary's lifeboat helped to refloat a full-rigged ship, but in vain, for after being towed clear, she developed extensive leaks and foundered in deep water. The *Horsa*, of Liverpool, laden with grain, was attempting to beat round St. Martin's Head when she 'missed stays' and to avoid running on the rocks was headed for Bread and Cheese Cove, a comparatively sheltered, but rocky bay. The lifeboat was launched in response to a phone message from the St. Martin's coastguard, and quickly reached the scene. As the tide had fallen, the *Horsa* was then hard aground. Her master asked the lifeboat to land his wife and child, and the child's nurse, as a precautionary measure, and to call a tug. Several lifeboatmen went on board to help prepare a towing hawser which was later passed to the steam packet *Lyonesse*, when the tide began flowing. They had little difficulty in getting the *Horsa* away from the shore, but the tow parted three times in the confused seas, and some unsuspected damage below the waterline caused her to fill so quickly that she had to be abandoned sixteen miles west of the Bishop. The *Lyonesse* brought the whole crew back to St. Mary's.

In 1899 St. Mary's was provided with a Watson type sailing lifeboat of the same length as the previous self-righter. She was a fine boat of a fine class and was also named *Henry Dundas*, the fourth of the name. During 1899-1900 the present lifeboat house and slip were built at Carn Thomas, on the east side of the harbour, at a cost of £1,600. It was largely rebuilt in 1914 for the motor lifeboat, and has been improved and enlarged from time to time.

On June 22nd 1901, the four-masted barque *Falkland*, of Liverpool, bound with wheat from Tacoma for Falmouth, for orders, was taken too close to the Islands by a moderate S.S.W. gale, with heavy seas and thick weather. After fighting for two hours to keep out of danger, she came too close to a reef, and, on being put aback, was driven stern first on to the Bishop Rock, coming in so close that her mainyard struck the lighthouse tower. A boat was immediately lowered and took in 27, including the Captain's wife and baby. The *Falkland* drifted northwards, but was filling faster than was expected and she suddenly foundered in deep water, six men being drowned as they attempted to launch the second boat. The St. Agnes lifeboat found the first boat and, taking some on board, towed it to St. Mary's. Meanwhile the St. Mary's lifeboat made an unsuccessful search for further survivors. The barque's figurehead is one of the many in the 'Valhalla' at Tresco Abbey.

Both the lifeboats were engaged on September 20th 1903 in what turned out to be one of the classic cases of salvage by the Islanders. The steel barque *Queen Mab*, of Glasgow, bound with fustic logwood from Punta Arenas for Falmouth, for orders, was making to anchor in the Roads to await a favourable wind. However, the easterly breeze was not strong enough to drive her quickly through St. Mary's Sound and, making leeway, she touched the Spanish Ledges. She began to leak badly, and when the lifeboats arrived, their crews were immediately engaged to man the pumps. The gig *O. and M.* put a pilot on board and was asked to land the Captain's wife and child. She then returned to help, and the crew of the gig *Leo* of St. Mary's were also engaged. The barque limped into the Roads and anchored as well as she could, in a position rather too close to the tail of Samson. Urgent messages were sent for the steam packet *Lyonesse*, but she was aground at the Pier and would not float on the tide for two or three hours. There was no option but to carry on pumping and for seven hours the men stuck at the task, augmenting the ship's pumps with a force pump from the *Lyonesse*, taken out in a gig. When eventually the steamer floated, her steam already boosted, she got to the scene in double quick time, and found the situation fairly desperate. Unfortunately the master of the *Queen Mab* had little faith in the power of the steamer and delayed slipping his anchors, so that the first warp broke and time was wasted in manoeuvring to take the strain while avoiding the nearby rocks. After a couple of anxious hours the barque was brought into the harbour as far as the steamer dared run into the shallow water, complicated by the presence of a large number of French fishing vessels. By some mischance the barque was not properly secured, and she drifted out a short distance, not being brought alongside the quay until a further tide had passed. Later, at low water, holes in the bows were patched, and she was eventually towed to Havre to discharge her cargo. Some useful sums were awarded the owners of the *Lyonesse* and to the crews of the gig and lifeboats for their work.

In 1904 St. Agnes asked for a larger boat and they chose one of the Liverpool type, this being more stable than the former self-righter. Due to the crew position, however, she still had to be 10-oared, rather than 12-oared as at St. Mary's. She was named *Charles Deere James*, being given by a lady who wished to remain anonymous, although after her death she was revealed as Mrs. S. C. Guthrie, of Tunbridge Wells. Five years later this boat was changed for a Watson of similar size, and with the same name, but meanwhile she had been involved in one of the most tragic of this century's wrecks in the Islands.

On December 13th 1907, the huge steel seven-masted schooner *Thomas W. Lawson*, of Boston—the first and last of her kind, and one of the wonders of the contemporary shipping world—was bound with petroleum in barrels from Philadelphia for London. In a rising gale, the weather thick with rain, she found herself heading inside the Bishop Rock, and at about 4 p.m. had to anchor to ride out the storm. Both lifeboats went off and reached her soon after dark. Her master would not abandon ship as the anchors were then holding, but was grateful for the offer of a pilot, and William J. Hicks boarded her from the St. Agnes lifeboat. Normally the lifeboats would not have entertained the idea of leaving a vessel in this position and in the prevailing weather, but two unfortunate incidents occurred. First, in manoeuvring close enough to hail, the St. Mary's boat struck the schooner's stern, carrying away her own mast. The schooner Captain sent her back to telegraph for a tug from Falmouth, and to have an opportunity to carry out repairs, Then one of the St. Agnes crew collapsed, possibly with a heart attack, and to save his life they returned to station with him, having first arranged a recall signal for use if necessary, the Captain again declining an offer to land his crew at the same time. As a further link in the chain of mishaps, the St. Agnes crew did not notify St. Mary's that they had left the schooner, thinking the other boat would be disabled by loss of her mast. In fact the St. Mary's men had immediately set to work and had their boat ready again by midnight. During the night the gale increased and gusted to ninety miles per hour, causing terrific seas. In these circumstances, it is quite probable the lifeboats would not have been able to stand by in any case. Some time after 3 a.m., the schooner's cables parted and she drove rapidly on to Minmanueth. On striking, most of the crew took to the masts, but she split in two and then rapidly broke up. At dawn the weather had moderated and the lifeboats, not having had recall signals, went out expecting to be able to help the *Lawson* to safety, but they found nothing but vast quantities of wreckage floating in a sea of oil. Other boats also put out to search the area. The gig *Slippen* found a man alive on Annet, but he was so badly injured he died soon afterwards. The Captain and engineer were washed on to Hellweather and were so exhausted that they lapsed into unconsciousness, not being able to make their presence known until a further day had passed. They were, in fact, saved at considerable risk by the *Slippen's* crew, and by Frederick C. Hicks gallantly swimming a deep gully between two reefs to take a rope to the Captain. He was a son of the W. J. Hicks who had been put on board as a pilot, but who was among the fifteen lost. F. C. Hicks was awarded the Silver Medal of the R.N.L.I., and a gold watch by the United States Government for his exploit, while the whole gig's crew received U.S. Gold Medals. The Captain of the *Lawson* later told of the gallant efforts W. J. Hicks had made to save his vessel after the cables parted, but there were insufficient sails left to carry her on course, and no boats, for she had passed through very severe weather on her passage across the Atlantic.

Remembering the earlier loss of the barque *Minnehaha*, it was a strange coincidence that the Atlantic liner of the same name should strand in the Scillies, but almost by a miracle she survived to steam again. It was at 1.30 a.m. on April 18th 1910, that the coast guard reported a vessel firing guns west of Bryher, and the Bishop light-keepers heard them at the same time. Although the sea was smooth it was foggy, and it transpired that the liner, of 13,433 tons, bound from New York for London with 66 passengers, a large crew, a general cargo, and more than 230 cattle, had been set northward by the currents and narrowly escaped striking Shipman Head at the northern tip of Bryher. They had managed to sheer away but came the wrong side of Scilly Rock and struck the reef on its south-east side. Although the seas remained comparatively calm and she did not seem to be badly holed, there was the imminent possibility of her sliding off the rock and being thrown on her beam ends. The Bryher men knew exactly where to go, and while the St. Mary's lifeboat was picking her way through the fog and searching for the casualty, they landed the passengers and stewardesses in their gigs. The crew and cattle-men were still on board, however, and the lifeboat was asked to stand by. The fog lifted with the light and later two Falmouth tugs arrived, part of the crew being transferred to one of them. When the returning tide made it evident the liner would stay upright, the master told the lifeboatmen to go and get some rest. Salvage took three weeks, during which time all but ten of the cattle were saved by swimming to Samson. The liner company was generous to the Bryher people, who also had additional 'fringe benefits' in collecting the varied and mostly useful cargo which was jettisoned, most of it washing up in Hell Bay.

Both lifeboats were called on January 8th 1911, to the ship *Ardencraig*, of Glasgow, which struck the Gunners, but immediately drifted off. She was laden with grain from Melbourne for Cardiff, 101 days out, and had a crew of 31. There was dense fog when she struck, but it cleared to show her drifting in a sinking state with her foreyards aback, and her crew in their boats nearby. The St. Agnes lifeboat reached the scene first and took on board eight men from one boat, put a lifeboatman on another boat, and took her in tow. It was too dangerous to board the ship as she already had nine feet of water in her holds, but the master asked the lifeboats to stand by in case he could re-board. However, about an hour later, she suddenly rolled over to port and sank bows first. The rest of the crew were towed in by a light-house tender. The *Ardencraig* was another of the many victims of the northward current, her master imagining himself at least twenty miles to the south-west.

In dense fog, at 4.30 on the afternoon of June 23rd 1914, another large Atlantic liner found herself among the deadly rock pinnacles in the western approaches, and she struck Zantman's Rock before she could be extricated. She was the Red Star liner *Gothland*, 7,660 tons, bound from Montreal for Rotterdam with 84 passengers, mostly rejected emigrants in very straitened circumstances, together with a crew of about 170. Wireless was used to make the casualty known, possibly its first use in this area, the messages coming back from Land's End Wireless Station by telegraph via Penzance. The steam packet *Lyonesse* towed out the St. Mary's lifeboat, and picked up the St. Agnes lifeboat on the way. Mr. Mumford's motor boat also went out. While launching one of the ship's boats, with 42 passengers, it fell from the davits and was smashed, but fortunately the St. Mary's lifeboat was nearby. Coxswain James Lethbridge sprang on to the sinking boat and assisted the women and children into the lifeboat. By 9.30 p.m. the operation was complete, the St. Mary's lifeboat having taken off 81, and the St. Agnes 71, most of whom had been transferred to the more comfortable quarters on the *Lyonesse*. As the Captain and some of the crew wished to stay on board the *Gothland*, the St. Agnes lifeboat stood by throughout the night. The liner was in a precarious position but fortunately the June weather was kind and she was later refloated, after much of her grain and frozen meat cargo had been jettisoned.

During the First World War the St. Agnes lifeboat made many useful rescues, but it so happened the St. Mary lifeboat made none. First there was the steamer *Sola*, of Stavanger, torpedoed by a German submarine, in spite of her neutral colours, when some 82 miles from land. The crew took to their boats and sailed for 48 hours before being seen on October 26th 1916, about three miles off the Scillies. The *Charles Deere James* put off and brought them in from almost certain death, for in their exhausted state they would have had great difficulty in picking a course to safety among the rocks.

Next, the St. Agnes lifeboat played a part in a drama of treachery which, at a time when relations between Germany and the neutral European countries were already strained, caused a tremendous stir. Seven Dutch and one Norwegian steamers, which had been sheltering at Falmouth, left in company and were torpedoed by a German submarine on February 22nd 1917, in the English Channel approaches, without the warning and examination of papers required by International Law. One, the *Menado*, of Rotterdam, was towed back to Falmouth by a trawler, but six Dutch vessels of 4,000-7,000 tons, the *Eemland*, *Bandoeng*, *Gaasterland*, *Jacatra*, *Noorderdijk* and *Zaandijk*, were sunk. Some of the survivors approached the Islands in their boats and were seen by the Bishop light-keepers, who at once signalled for the lifeboat. The *Charles Deere James* went off and found two boats full of men. A lifeboatman was put in each to pilot them to safety, and she then searched farther afield, finding one more boat, bringing the total of men saved to 47. The Netherlands Section of the League of Neutral Countries afterwards awarded a specially inscribed medal to each of the lifeboat crew, as well as to the crews of several trawlers engaged in search and rescue farther afield.

Less than a month later, on March 13th, the lifeboat was again called out by signals from the Bishop and found two boats with 26 men from the steamer *Algonquin*, of New York, which had been torpedoed. Again on June 2nd of the same year she went off to bring in the exhausted crew of the French barque *Jean Cordonnier*, torpedoed 39 hours previously. The final service came as the war was drawing to its close. On October 1st 1918, they launched at first light to seek a boat reported by the Bishop look-out, and found six men. Of these five were wounded.

two seriously, their four-masted schooner, the *Atlantico*, bound from Newport for Oporto with coal, having been sunk by gunfire. The men were quickly landed to receive medical attention, and later the lifeboat went off again, finding a further boat which contained three, one of whom was wounded.

This proved to be the last service of the St. Agnes lifeboats. Partly because a motor lifeboat had been sent to St. Mary's, and partly because it was difficult to get sufficient men for a crew, the station was closed in 1920.

The motor lifeboat at St. Mary's was the gift of the Right Hon. Arnold Morley, one-time M.P. for Nottingham, and Postmaster-General, and was named *Elsie*, after his wife. The station had been earmarked for a motor lifeboat as early as 1913, and although the Morley gift was made in 1916, there were delays in building caused by the war, and she did not arrive until October 1919. She was of the very successful and sturdy 45ft. Watson type, with a 60 h.p. Tyler engine. She started her career with a couple of 'ambulance' services, landing a sick light-keeper from the Bishop, and then taking a sick man to Penzance for urgent hospital treatment. Since motor lifeboats have been stationed in island communities around our coasts, this type of service has been frequent, there having been twenty or so to date at St. Mary's, usually performed in conditions which had stopped the crossing of the normal mail steamer. Anyone who knows the 'flower ships' will understand that this means extremely bad weather.

The *Elsie's* first important service was on December 2nd 1920, when she saved 24 from the steamer *Hathor*, of Hamburg. This vessel had been interned in Chile during the war, was recommissioned after the armistice, and sent home. Her engines had broken down a week or so earlier and two tugs had been towing her from the Azores, but when they were off the Islands a violent gale had blown up and the tow parted. Drifting towards St. Agnes the *Hathor* dropped anchors, but they did not hold and she eventually ran foul of Lethegus. The situation was extremely dangerous and two boats hurriedly left the ship with 19 men. These were taken in by the lifeboat, but five more were still to be saved. The *Hathor* was lying head to the gale and afforded no shelter whatever for coming alongside. It was a situation where a motor lifeboat could perform a miracle which would have been denied a pulling boat. Manoeuvring delicately with her powerful engine, violently rising and falling on the waves, she nosed up to the towering steel hull. The remaining men dropped down one by one as opportunity presented, but there were several collisions and the lifeboat herself did not escape damage. One man fell between the ships, but was saved by the presence of mind of Bob Ellis, who quickly thrust a large bundle over the side to act as a fender. Later he realised that the bundle contained the ship's papers and chronometer.

On July 11th 1921, there was an unusual call to a steamship on fire west of the Bishop. The *Western Front*, of Seattle, bound from Jacksonville for London and Hamburg, had caught alight after a mysterious explosion. One of the Island mail steamers, the *Peninnis*, had gone to her aid and taken on board 40 men and the Captain's wife. She then attempted to tow the steamer with a view to saving her by beaching, but the tow rope parted and fouled her own screw, so that she was herself in grave danger with her flaming tow closing in on her and being unable to get clear. The lifeboat took in the rescued persons, of whom the Captain's wife and eight others had been injured in the fire, and one had died. The blazing hulk was later sunk by a destroyer as a danger to navigation.

The lifeboat crew had a long ordeal on July 8th 1922, when they were called out during a S.W. gale of exceptional violence following a distress message from the steamer *Concordia*, of Genoa, which had broken her propeller shaft near the Wolf light-house, some 20 miles east of the Islands. After plunging into the seas for three hours the lifeboat's engine spluttered to a stop and all efforts failed to get it going again. In the prevailing weather it was impossible to open the hatch to the engine room, and the only course open was to set sail and run before the gale to Falmouth. She was not fitted with wireless and as the hours passed considerable anxiety was felt for her safety, moreover her crew could not have the satisfaction of being told that the Penlee lifeboat had reached the casualty and was standing by. The *Elsie* eventually arrived at Falmouth 14½ hours after her launch, Coxswain James Lethbridge being at the wheel the whole time. Eventually she got back to St. Mary's at midnight on the 10th, after further vicissitudes, more than 56 hours after launching. In recognition of the seamanship and endurance displayed, the Thanks inscribed on Vellum were awarded to Coxswain Lethbridge, and extra monetary awards made to the crew.

The greatest rescue of modern times in the Islands was that from the wreck of the steamer *Isabo*, of Lussin-Piccolo, Italy, on October 27th 1927. Besides *Elsie* and her gallant crew, many island boats were involved and the Life-boat Institution awarded two Silver Medals, six

Bronze Medals, and several Vellums, while the Italian Government sent 38 Silver and Bronze Medals. Poor guide to heroism though they are, this impressive list at least shows that the whole resources of the community were mobilised to perfect this rescue. There is room here only for a summary of the main events.

The *Isabo*, 6,827 tons, with wheat, ran ashore at 5 p.m. on the north side of Scilly Rock, the stark and dangerous outpost west of Bryher. She must have been driven northwards from her correct course, like so many before her, but the immediate cause of the disaster was thick fog. There was a moderate S.W. breeze and soon afterwards this developed into a gale which increased and, incidentally, caused widespread damage in the south and west of the country during the next two days. The *Isabo's* siren was heard on Bryher, and three boats immediately put off to see what they could do. They were the old but oft-proven gig *Czar*; the motor boats *Sunbeam* and *Ivy*. The *Czar* was handled by a crew who knew their drill to perfection and who were no doubt inspired by the great gig rescues of the past. It was by now quite dark and the fog was still dense. The dangers were obvious and well known to them, but with a light boat under oars they had distinct advantages over motor boats among the rocks and expanses of floating weed in the area. To this was added the hazard of floating grain from the wreck which threatened to clog the water circulating systems of the motor boats and did, in fact, make the *Ivy's* engine glow red hot by the time she returned. The *Czar* first came across men floating on pieces of wreckage—hatch covers, spars, iron tanks, and the like, and, tossing dangerously in the wash and backwash among the rocks, they picked up eleven before hailing the *Ivy* and transferring them to make room for more. They picked up three more from the sea and then, hearing cries from the wreck, which they found had broken in two at the bridge, they managed to get a line on board by which means one more was dragged through the water to safety. The *Ivy*, besides taking in the eleven from the *Czar*, found another man and saved him. All the rescued were practically naked and suffering much from the cold, so, the lifeboat having now come to the scene, the *Czar* and *Ivy* made for Bryher where the rescued were skilfully attended. Meanwhile the *Sunbeam* had approached by a different route round the north of Bryher, and picked up one man from the water. The mass of debris made it impracticable to approach the wreck, so they launched a 9ft. dinghy which they had brought, and while four men stayed in the motor boat, Charles Jenkins and Edward R. Jenkins pulled towards the wreck,

The full-rigged ship Horsa *aground off St Martin's, Isles of Scilly, April 4th 1893. The St Mary's lifeboat is alongside and a typical pilot gig pulling away. The* Horsa *was towed off but later foundered in deep water (Photo: Gibson)*

The liner Minnehaha (*13433 tons*) *ashore on Bryher, Isles of Scilly, April 18th 1910. No lives were lost and the cattle she carried were also saved by swimming them (below) to temporary pasture on Samson (Photo: Gibson)*

The St Agnes lifeboat Charles Deere James *pulling to the* Ardencraig, *January 8th 1911, shortly before the latter foundered off the Gunners, Isles of Scilly*

The s.s. Castleford *ashore on the Western Rocks, Isles of Scilly, June 9th 1887. Her crew of 25 were rescued by the St Mary's lifeboat (Photo: Gibson)*

The St Mary's lifeboat Elsie *towing the Lowestoft steam drifter* Lord Haldane *off Steval, March 20th 1929 (Photo: Gibson)*

The collier Llandaff *(397 tons) at Nanjizal Bay, Land's End, in 1889. In ballast from Sheerness to Cardiff, she went ashore in fog but was later re-floated. In 1899 she was again ashore on the Cornish coast, on Bude breakwater (see illustration in Vol. 1) (Photo: Gibson)*

The s.s. Wimborne *(3466 tons) wrecked under Carn Barra Point, near Land's End, November 7th 1910. All 27 aboard her were rescued by rocket apparatus from the forward part of the vessel, seen here, the stern half having already broken up*

disregarding the extreme danger on all sides, and having to bail out frequently. In each of three sorties they took in one man, each having to be hauled carefully over the stern to avoid capsizing the boat. While this was going on the *Sunbeam* picked up another man, and then, hearing cries from the wreck, they found a way to her stern, threw a line on board, and by this means drew through the sea seven more, including Captain A. Tarabocchia. They then returned to Bryher to land the rescued.

The lifeboat was launched in eight minutes from the alarm call, and having crossed the Roads began threading through the Neck of Gerwick towards Scilly Rock, a feat difficult enough in daylight and calm weather, but in growing darkness, fog and high seas, one to make the stoutest heart hesitate. Not knowing precisely where the wreck was lying, they spent some time searching until they fell in with the *Ivy* and obtained full information. Arriving on the scene about 9 p.m., they found men were clinging to the foremast, but the situation of the wreck among the rocks and in the prevailing weather was such that Coxswain Lethbridge had to make a difficult decision. It is probable that, had the rescue been attempted there and then, the lifeboat would have herself been wrecked. It was decided to wait until dawn, and the lifeboat went round Shipman Head to shelter in New Grimsby, until the time was ripe. During the night Doctor W. E. Ivers came over from St. Mary's and offered to accompany the lifeboat. They set out to be near the *Isabo* at dawn and were glad to hear cries for help which showed there was still a chance to save life. Heavy seas were breaking over the wreck, and at times even over the men in the rigging. They approached the lee side and fired a line from the gun. The first line was blown clear. The second straddled the steamer, but the crew were too exhausted to reach it. A third fell near the group, but a man trying to secure it was washed overboard. They went full speed ahead towards him and fortunately retrieved him, deeply unconscious, but floating on his lifejacket. Two other men slid down the rigging but were washed overboard before they could use the line and again the lifeboat successfully dashed to save them. These men made it known that the fourth on the mast was dead. Shouts were then heard from a rock and they fired a line to a lone figure, naked save for his lifejacket. He fell into the sea when attempting to reach the line, but swam powerfully towards the lifeboat and was dragged in. They could see no more survivors and returned to Bryher to land the four men who were understandably exhausted and numb after their ordeal. A further search was made later in the morning, but no more were found. By then it had been ascertained that six were missing, three of whom were probably drowned in the stokehold when she struck.

On Boxing Day in the same year of 1927 a service was carried out in unusual circumstances. Shortly before noon, watchers at St. Mary's saw a large barge-type vessel approaching the Islands and having the spritsail rig more often seen at the opposite end of the English Channel than in these waters. Most of her sails were in shreds, but she appeared to have a man aboard with local knowledge, for she tacked through Crow Sound, across the Bar and towards Tresco with hardly a move miscalculated. However, when she made no attempt to round to her anchor, but made for the land, it was realised something was amiss. The lifeboat was launched and caught up with her just after she had grounded on the sandy foreshore. Then it was found there was not a soul on board except a canary, singing bravely in its cage. The bird was brought ashore and later the *Lady Daphne*, of Rochester, was refloated and towed to Falmouth for repairs. It transpired that she had been making for Plymouth from the Thames, with bricks and tiles, but the skipper was washed overboard in dirty weather off Plymouth. The other two hands could do nothing to stop her driving down Channel before the gale. They burned flares, and when they had lit their very last drop of paraffin they were seen from the Lizard. The Lizard lifeboat raced after them, eventually catching them twelve miles out, and made an extremely skilful rescue, having to leave the barge to its fate.

In 1930 a new motor lifeboat, slightly larger than her predecessor, and of the latest Watson cabin type, was sent to St. Mary's. She was the *Cunard*, gift of the well known steamship company. This class of boat could travel 116 miles at full speed without refuelling, and take in 95 persons in rough weather. For her first service on April 13th 1932, she towed the French fishing vessel *Yvonne et Marie* off rocks in the New Grimsby Channel between Tresco and Bryher, but her first real test came when the schooner *Mynonie R. Kirby*, sensationally labelled a 'Treasure Ship' in the popular press, was dismasted off the Islands.

This fine old schooner was one of the formerly numerous Portmadoc slate carriers, dating from 1878 and having had a full and strenuous life. She had been purchased by some enthusiasts in escapism and fitted out for a trip to the South Seas to seek adventure and fortune. She is reported to have had stores for five years, filming equipment, barter goods, and no less than 300 rifles with ammunition to suit. On November 25th 1933, she left Falmouth with a fair wind for her first port of call—Gibraltar. The next day, when they were sixty miles west of Ushant, the weather freshened and, while she laboured in heavy swells, both the fore and main masts snapped off close to the deck. Fortunately, an Egyptian steamer, the *Star of Ramleh*, sighted her early on the next day, and took her in tow towards Falmouth, covering 110 miles before the tow-rope parted in the early evening. The tow was taken over by the Dutch salvage tug *Zwarte Zee*, but in an increasing S.E. gale she again broke adrift, tearing out her capstan. With both masts trailing over the side, her small auxiliary engine out of order, and her anchors down but dragging, the schooner was in a sorry predicament. They were then about five miles west of Peninnis Head and the tug wirelessed to St. Mary's for the lifeboat, as she could not launch her own boats in the prevailing conditions. It so happened the Coxwain and Second Coxswain were away in England visiting their father, a former Coxswain, who was dangerously ill. The Bowman, Harry Barrett, took charge, and they launched at about 2 p.m. A revised position was signalled from St. Agnes, which told them they had to travel about ten miles dead into the wind and seas. This took about two hours. The tug soon became visible, but the wreck, lying low in the water, without a single spar standing, was out of sight in the troughs until they were almost on her. Owing to the mass of wreckage, to go alongside was out of the question. They fired a line from the gun and it was seized. However, there was nothing high enough on the wreck to which they could fasten it and use it in the correct way, so a single line had to be hauled backwards and forwards with the buoy. Since both wreck and lifeboat were drifting, much manoeuvring of engines was necessary to keep the line as taut as possible. The first man dragged through the sea brought with him a small dog wrapped in a pillow case and carefully held high over his head. Then, with intervals for tightening or unhitching the line, all six were passed across, the operation taking nearly three hours. For a smart service carried out in abnormal conditions, the acting Coxswain, Harry Barrett, was awarded the Bronze Medal of the Institution, the motor mechanic, J. H. Rokahr, the Record of Thanks on Vellum, and special letters of thanks to the other six of the crew. Next day they launched again to try to locate the derelict schooner as she was a grave danger to navigation. She had drifted well away, however, and they did not find her, but there were reports of sightings, the last on December 4th.

The second World War gave St. Mary's lifeboat a fairly busy time. The first war launch took place on October 13th 1939, when she was called to an R.A.F. flying boat which had come down some fifty miles to the west. Fortunately the crew were saved by a Dutch steamer and the *Cunard* was recalled after going only a short way. All told there were eleven wartime launches, most of them searches for vessels or aircraft without result. Three times, however, there was the satisfaction of a skilfully accomplished rescue.

The first of these, on December 22nd 1939, was not actually a war service, but the casualty was caused by the prevailing black-out conditions and radio silence. The Clyde Steamship Company's steamer *Longships*, bound from Belfast for Plymouth with a general cargo and crew of 27, ran on to the Seven Stones. She quickly broke her back in that exposed position, and at about 5.30 p.m. when the lifeboat came on the scene, there was no question of salvage. The crew were taken off and brought back to St. Mary's.

A service on November 14th 1943 entailed probably the shortest journey ever travelled by the St. Mary's lifeboat on a rescue mission. Soon after eight in the evening the commander of a naval motor launch reported to the Coxswain that a landing craft, which had just come in from Gibraltar, was ashore at Newford Island. There was a fresh wind and rough sea. A morse signal was sent to ascertain if help was needed, and they asked for the lifeboat to stand by in case the craft capsized. On arriving at the scene, the crew were ready to leave, and all 17 were brought back to the Pier, the service taking less than an hour. On the same day three similar landing craft sank in high seas off the Lizard.

The final war service took place on January 12th 1945. Three days earlier the United States Government transport *Jonas Lie*, a 'Liberty Ship', had been torpedoed in the eastern Atlantic. Her crew had been taken off, but a salvage party of fifteen was on board as she had been in tow of a tug. Now, however, the tow had parted and she was wallowing helplessly in the swell some four miles north of Round Island. The *Cunard* was called out at 9.45 p.m., and to quote the official account—'The night was exceptionally dark, with a north-east gale and very rough sea'. They went through the North-West Channel and passed to the west of the off-lying rocks. 'It was a difficult and dangerous piece of navigation without lights or marks'. They were on the scene in two hours and it took about half an houı to take off the crew. 'She returned by a shorter and more hazardous route, arriving at five on the 13th'. In recognition of the skilful navigation displayed on this occasion the Institution awarded its Thanks on Vellum to both Coxswain Matthew Lethbridge and Second Coxswain James T. Lethbridge.

In the ten years after the war, the *Cunard* continued to perform valuable service to a variety of vessels, a French and a Faroese fishing boat, a British steam coaster, several local craft, including the mail packet *Scillonian*, which grounded in fog on Wingletang Ledge, and the launch *Kittern*, which was disabled while landing passengers on the same occasion.

A notable service of this period was in helping to save the London steamer *Duke of Sparta*, 5,400 tons, from the Seven Stones. She was in ballast, bound from Liverpool for London, and was making water, but fortunately could control it with her pumps. She refloated without help, but was then in the middle of the series of reefs and without the help of the lifeboat, which took soundings, and boarded her Second Coxswain as a pilot, she would probably have come to further harm if left to her own devices. With a typically friendly gesture the lifeboat called at the light-ship on the way back and collected their mail.

A fine service, for which Coxswain Lethbridge was awarded the Bronze Medal, took place on the evening of January 21st 1955. The Panamanian steamer *Mando*, 7,176 tons, bound from Hampton Roads for Rotterdam with coal, when coming from the Atlantic in dense fog, found herself among the rocks at the north of the Scillies and struck part of the Golden Ball reef near Men-a-Vaur. She sounded her siren, which was heard by the Round Island light keepers, who then radioed a distress message. No less than seven large steamers and motor ships in the area altered course to help, but in view of her position it was as well that they did not approach too closely. The *Cunard* was launched just after 9 p.m., which, being close to low water, precluded their taking the sheltered passage between Tresco and Bryher. With the fog and darkness, which brought visibility down to as little as fifty feet in places, it was necessary to rely largely on the compass and occasional glimpses of the rocks. They went west of Samson and White Island, then through Castle Bryher Neck, between Gweal and Scilly Rock, and passed the northern tip of Bryher. After about an hour's run they approached Men-a-vaur and saw flares from the casualty. The *Mando* had launched two boats, which were lying on her lee side, and these complicated the business of taking off the crew, but the *Cunard* found a position in which to lie, rising and falling on the swell, using the engines as necessary, while 24 men came down a ladder. The master wished to remain on board in case there came a chance to save the vessel, but fortunately they were able to persuade him to leave. The two boats, containing the crew's effects, were taken in tow, also the 30ft. gig *Sussex* (a veteran of many rescues), which had put off from Bryher. Returning through New Grimsby channel, they waited a couple of hours for the tide to make and took the opportunity of taking the crew's belongings into the lifeboat, leaving the ship's boats to the Bryher men. By then the fog had lifted considerably and they arrived back at St. Mary's about half past midnight on the 22nd.

The same year of 1955 was a busy one for the St. Mary's crew, and what turned out to be the last services of the *Cunard* were performed on July 22nd and 23rd to the Panamanian steamship *Punta*, 2,197 tons, which went aground in fog on the Seven Stones. The lifeboat was launched soon after 7 a.m., by which time the fog had lifted and there was a slight breeze, so that it took little more than half an hour to reach the scene. The *Punta* was loaded with phosphate rock and bound from Bougie (Algeria) for Portishead (Bristol) Dock. She had a crew of 25, and the master's wife. The heavy cargo had already had its effect and she was well aground forward, with a pronounced list to port, the rail being under water. Twenty of the crew were in two boats moored astern and these were first taken into the *Cunard*. The master and remaining four men were taken off the wreck and at their request the lifeboat stood by until low water to assess the damage and the chances of salvage. The French salvage tug *Abeille 26* came on the scene and in the evening the master of the *Punta* asked to be put on board the tug with his crew. This was done, but it was thought advisable for the lifeboat to remain standing by. Later the master of the salvage tug made a survey, with Captain Mathiases, and they decided it would be better to wait until next day before attempting to tow the *Punta* off the reef. Accordingly the lifeboat took twenty of the crew, including two Somali stowaways, to St. Mary's, together with their numerous pets—three cats, two linnets, a canary and a goldfinch. The next morning the Seven Stones light-vessel reported catching a glimpse of the casualty before fog again closed in, and that the situation appeared unchanged. However, when the *Abeille 26* pulled her free at the top of the tide, she immediately broke in two, sinking in deep water. The *Cunard* was then asked to bring ashore the master, his wife, and three who had stayed on the tug, and so, travelling again through dense fog, she made a second service run to the reef.

In December of that year, 1955, a lifeboat of the new 46ft. 9in. Watson class was sent to the station. Her cost, £32,000, was provided by an amalgamation of seven legacies. She was formally named *Guy and Clare Hunter* by Mrs. A. A. Dorrien Smith at a ceremony on June 20th

1956, and at the same time a Certificate of Service was presented to Coxswain Matthew Lethbridge, retiring after 31 years in charge, having won both the Silver and Bronze Medals for gallantry. The maiden service of the new lifeboat took place soon afterwards, on August 8th, when she towed home the local fishing boat *Corah*, disabled with a fouled propeller, with five visitors aboard.

After a number of similar services to both English and French fishing vessels and yachts, on May 15th 1958, the lifeboat herself suffered the indignity of being blown ashore at Porth Mellin during a 90 miles-an-hour gale. Fortunately, she narrowly missed some large boulders and came to rest undamaged on a sandy beach. She had been temporarily moored afloat while the house and slipway were being altered. On October 4th following, she saved the small motor yacht *Mary Ann*, of Aberstwyth, and her crew of two, after their rudder had broken while they were setting off on the long voyage to New Zealand.

Next, on April 26th 1959, the *Guy and Clare Hunter* saved a new motor tug in distress on her delivery voyage. The *Helen M. McAllister* had come from her builder's yard at Appledore, called for fuel at Falmouth and then set out for Montreal. She was only some 50 miles west of the Bishop when both her engines failed and, battered by heavy seas, she drifted eastwards for thirty hours until she was among the Islands. Both anchors were dropped, but one was lost and the other dragged. In the late afternoon of the 26th she burnt flares which were seen from St. Mary's and the lifeboat was launched. In spite of the westerly gale, they arrived in fifteen minutes and Coxswain Matthew Lethbridge, Jr., quickly appraised the situation. In response to his radio-telephone message a hawser was brought out in a launch, by which means the tug was towed to St. Mary's harbour.

There have since been a number of occasions when the lifeboat has been able to do service to small craft, but considerations of space forbid a full account. There have also been ambulance services, one unusual, in that it involved one of H.M. submarines. Dates and other details of services not fully described will be found in the Record of Services on another page.

BOAT RECORD, ISLES OF SCILLY

Years on Station	Length, Breadth, Depth	Type, Oars, Crew	Weight, Cost, O. No.	Built, Year, Builder	Boat's Name, Donor, Authority
St. Mary's lifeboats					
1837-					—
1840					Nat. Shipwreck Instn.
					N.S.I. and Coast Guard
1840-	26′		1t15	1828[1]	—
1855	8′ 6″	10	£150	Plenty,	N.S.I.
	3′		—	Newbury	N.S.I. and C.G.
1874-	37′	SR		1874	*Henry Dundas*
1890	9′	12	£438		Leg. Mrs. Dundas Drummond
					R.N.L.I.
1890-	42′	SR	7t7	1890	*Henry Dundas*
1891	11′	12	£667	Forrestt,	as above
			271	Limehouse	R.N.L.I.
1891-	38′	SR		1891	*Henry Dundas*
1899	8′	12	£609	Woolfe,	as above
			313	Shadwell	R.N.L.I.
1899-	38′	W	6t	1899	*Henry Dundas*
1919	9′ 4″	12	£856	Thames I.,	as above
			434	Blackwall	R.N.L.I.
1919-	45′	W(M)	15t	1919	*Elsie*
1930	12′ 6″	—	£6295	S. E. Saunders	Rt. Hon. Arnold Morley
		8	648	E. Cowes	R.N.L.I.
1930-	45′ 6″	WC(M)	19t15	1930	*Cunard*
1953	12′ 6″	—	£8324	Saunders-	Cunard Steamship Co. Ltd.
		8	728	Roe Cowes	R.N.L.I.
1955-	46′ 9″	W(M)	21t3	1955	*Guy and Clare Hunter*
	12′ 9″	—	£32103	White & Co.	Legs. Mrs. C. Hunter,
		8	926	Cowes	R.N.L.I. [Horncastle, and others
St. Agnes lifeboats					
1890-	34′	SR		1890	*James and Caroline*
1904	7′ 6″	10		Woolfe,	Leg. Jas. Goss, Stratford
			275	Shadwell	R.N.L.I. [Green
1904-	38′	L	4t3	1903	*Charles Deere James*
1909	10′	10		Thames I.,	Mrs. S. C. Guthrie,
			516	Blackwall	R.N.L.I. [Tunbridge Wells
1909-	38′	W	6t4	1909	*Charles Deere James*
1920	9′ 4″	10		Thames I.,	as above
			590	Blackwall	R.N.L.I.

1 Previously at Plymouth.

SERVICE RECORD, ST. MARY'S

Second Lifeboat				
1841	Jan.	4	p.s. *Thames*, of Dublin, helped to save 4 and landed 8 bodies	
Henry Dundas (I) Lifeboat				
1875	May	7	s.s. *Schiller*, of Hamburg, landed bodies and mail bags	
1880	Oct.	28	Brig *Messenger*, of Salcombe, stood by and saved	5
1881	Nov.	27	Barque *Excelsior*, of Hamburg, stood by	
1887	June	9	s.s. *Castleford*, of Liverpool, stood by and saved	25
Henry Dundas (II) Lifeboat				
1890	May	3	Brigantine *Antares*, of Nantes, saved vessel and	6
Henry Dundas (III) Lifeboat				
1893	Apr.	4	Ship *Horsa*, of Liverpool, landed 3 and assisted to save vessel	
1896	Dec.	15	Barque *Sophie*, of Frederickstadt, stood by abandoned vessel until moored	
Henry Dundas (IV) Lifeboat				
1900	Nov.	7	Barque *Dovre*, of Porsgrund, assisted to save vessel dismasted near Seven Stones	
1902	Feb.	1	Ketch *Ada*, of Gloucester, leaking at anchor in Sound, stood by	
		2	Brigantine *Lofaro*, of Naples, capsized and sank with all hands, unsuccessful search for survivors	
1903	Sept.	10	Small boat *Kathleen*, of St. Mary's, disabled in Crow Sound, landed 2	
		20	Barque *Queen Mab*, of Glasgow, assisted to save vessel	
1906	Aug.	21	s. trawler *Grassholm*, of South Shields, on Northern rocks, saved vessel	
1907	Dec.	13	7-masted Schooner *Thomas W. Lawson*, of Boston, brought ashore message for tug	
1910	Apr.	18	s.s. *Minnehaha*, of Belfast, stood by	
1911	Jan.	8	Ship *Ardencraig*, of Glasgow, stood by	
		12	Ketch *Georges*, of Auray, took doctor to St. Agnes to attend injured man	
1914	June	23	s.s. *Gothland*, of Antwerp, saved	81
Elsie Lifeboat				
1920	Mar.	8	Bishop Rock light-house, landed a sick keeper	
	Nov.	6	Took a sick man to Penzance, returned with the mails	
	Dec.	2	s.s. *Hathor*, of Hamburg, saved	24
1921	Feb.	2	Schooner *Leon Bonnat*, of Bayonne, wrecked on Crim, saved	12
	July	11	s.s. *Western Front*, of Seattle, landed 40 from s.s. *Peninnis*	
1922	Apr.	15	Ship *Pampa*, of Abo, dismasted south of St. Mary's, brought message for tug	
1925	Mar.	22	S. trawler *Cité de Verdun*, of Boulogne, wrecked Rosevear, saved	30
1927	Aug.	18	Motor fishing boat *Henrietta*, of St. Mary's, broken down in Sound, saved boat and	3
	Oct.	27	s.s. *Isabo*, of Lussin-Piccolo, saved	4
	Nov.	9	Schooner *Roscovite*, of Tréguier, disabled, saved vessel and	8
	Dec.	23	Schooner *Gougou*, of Vannes, dismasted near Seven Stones, saved	7
		26	Ketch-barge *Lady Daphne*, of Rochester, rendered assistance	
1928	Oct.	18	Took a sick girl to Penzance	
1929	Mar.	8	S. trawler *Rowland*, of Ostend, disabled, stood by while towed to Roads	
		20	S. drifter *Lord Haldane*, of Lowestoft, ashore Steval, saved vessel and	9

Cunard Lifeboat

1932	Apr.	13	Fishing vessel *Yvonne et Marie*, of Camaret, saved vessel	
1933	May	10	French fishermen stranded on Mincarlo, saved	4
	Aug.	27	Rowing boat of St. Mary's, saved boat and	2
	Nov.	28	Schooner *Mynonie R. Kirby*, of London, saved	6
1934	July	26	Bishop Rock light-house, brought back urgent message	
	Aug.	15	Motor boat *Penguin*, of St. Mary's, towed in boat and	3
1935	Apr.	7	Took a sick girl to Penzance	
	June	30	Motor fishing boat *Cambridge*, of St. Mary's, broken down, saved boat and	2
	Nov.	27	Took an injured man to Penzance	
1936	Jan.	9	Motor launch *Nor-nor*, of St. Mary's, disabled off St. Martin's, escorted launch to safety	
	Feb.	10	Took a doctor to St. Martin's	
		24	Took a sick man to Penzance	
1938	Feb.	13	S. trawler *Grosmont Castle*, of Swansea, lifeboat did not launch but medical advice given over radio-telephone	
	Sept.	17	Took a sick man to Penzance (ditto, Oct. 12)	
	Dec.	22	Steam dredger *Foremost 18*, of St. John, N.B., in difficulties near Spanish Ledges. Stood by until moored	
1939	Dec.	22	s.s. *Longships*, of Glasgow, saved	27
1943	Nov.	14	H.M. Landing Craft LC(T).354, saved	17
1945	Jan.	12	U.S. Transport *Jonas Lie*, saved	15
1946	Aug.	28	Motor fishing vessel *Capella*, of Thorshavn, escorted to safety vessel and 12	
1947	Apr.	8	Fishing vessel *Yvette*, of Camaret, ashore New Grimsby, landed 8	
		9	do. replaced crew	
	Oct.	4	s.s. *Radstock*, of Bridgwater, machinery breakdown off Round Island, saved vessel and	7
1948	Mar.	29	Fishing boat *Peaceful*, of St. Mary's, towed to anchorage	
	Apr.	19	s.s. *Duke of Sparta*, of London, assisted to save vessel	
	June	26	Fishing boat *Energetic*, of Porthleven, landed 1 man and a body from s.s. *Chrysanthystar*	
1951	Jan.	7	Bishop Rock light-house, landed a sick man	
	Sept.	10	s.s. *Scillonian*, of Scilly, landed 30 and gave help	
			M. launch *Kittern*, of Scilly, towed in disabled launch	
1952	May	17	M. launch *Gannet*, of Scilly, towed in launch and	7
1953	Sept.	8	Sailing dinghy, saved dinghy and	2
1955	Jan.	21	s.s. *Mando*, of Panama, saved	25
1955	Feb.	5	H.M. Tug *Warden*, landed 4 injured men	
	Mar.	23	Fishing boat *Reine de la Mer*, of Douarnenez, towed vessel and 16 to harbour from Porthcressa	
	July	22	s.s. *Punta*, of Panama, gave help and landed 20	
		23	do. landed 5 from a tug	

Guy and Clare Hunter Lifeboat

1956	Aug.	8	Fishing boat *Corah*, of St. Mary's, fouled propeller off Samson, towed in boat and landed 5	
		17	Fishing boat *Erin*, of St. Mary's, engine breakdown, towed in boat from Tresco and landed 5	
1957	Aug.	10	Two sailing dinghies, landed 4	
			Motor launch *Dawn*, of Tresco, broken down, saved launch and	8
1958	June	25	Fishing vessel *Meduce*, of Brest, broken down, saved vessel and	4
	Sept.	27	Fishing vessel *Pamela*, of Tresco, assisted owner to land	
	Oct.	4	Motor yacht *Mary Ann*, of Aberystwyth, rudder broken, saved yacht and	2

1959	Apr.	26	M. tug *Helen M. McAllister*, of Montreal, saved tug and	9
1960	Dec.	17	Brought doctor from Penzance	
1961	Mar.	9	Trawler *Petit Jean Yves*, ashore Gugh, landed 5	
		10	do. refloated vessel and escorted to harbour	
	June	28	Trawler *Enfant des Houles*, stood by while helicopter removed sick man	
	Aug.	11	Fishing boat *Mary Ann*, of St. Mary's, towed in boat and	1
	Oct.	31	Motor boat *Mab*, of St. Mary's, escorted boat to harbour	
1962	Jan.	6	Took sick man to Penzance	
1963	June	7	Motor boat *Phantee*, of St. Mary's, broken down, towed in boat and 2	
	Oct.	6	Trawler *Ketty et Michou*, put pilot and doctor on board	
	Dec.	14	Yacht *Searigs*, of Lymington, saved yacht and	2
1964	Jan.	6	m.v. *Eva Jeannette*, of Stockholm, landed an injured man	
Reserve Lifeboats.			(a) *C.D.E.C.* (b) *John R. Webb*	
1959	May	29	(a) Trawler *José Ramón*, of San Sebastian, assisted to save vessel and	13
1960	June	2	(b) H.M. Submarine *Trump*, took out doctors, landed captain and injured man, reboarded captain	

SERVICE RECORD, ST. AGNES

James and Caroline Lifeboat				
1891	Mar.	10	Smack *Porth*, of Padstow, saved	3
1892	Feb.	28	Smack *Jessie*, of Plymouth, moored vessel in safety	
		29	do. brought vessel into harbour	
1896	Nov.	29	Schooner *Ocean Belle*, of Beaumaris, dismasted, saved	3
1897	Sept.	29	s.s. *Starlight*, of West Hartlepool, stood by until out of danger	
	Dec.	25	Iron barge *100*, parted from tow, assisted to save barge	
1898	May	26	Lugger *Nyanza*, of Penzance, ashore Crebawethan, saved	4
1899	Mar.	21	Lugger *Lydia*, of Porthleven, dismasted near Bartholomew Ledge, assisted to save vessel	
1901	June	22	Barque *Falkland*, of Liverpool, saved a ship's boat and	27
1903	Sept.	20	Barque *Queen Mab*, of Glasgow, assisted to save vessel	
Charles Deere James (I) Lifeboat				
1907	Dec.	13	Seven-masted schooner *Thomas W. Lawson*, of Boston, boarded pilot	
Charles Deere James (II) Lifeboat				
1911	Jan.	8	Ship *Ardencraig*, of Glasgow, saved	15
1913	Nov.	28	Ship *Thornliebank*, of Glasgow, saved a ship's boat and	25
1914	June	23	s.s. *Gothland*, of Antwerp, saved	71
1916	Oct.	26	s.s. *Sola*, of Stavanger, saved	13
1917	Feb.	23	s.s. *Bandoeng*, of Rotterdam; s.s. *Eemland*, of Amsterdam; s.s. *Gaasterland*, of Rotterdam; s.s. *Jacatra*, of Rotterdam; s.s. *Noorderdijk*, of Rotterdam; s.s. *Zaandijk*, of Rotterdam — Vessels sunk by German submarine saved 3 boats and	47
	Mar.	13	s.s. *Algonquin*, of New York, landed from two boats	26
	June	2	Barque *Jean Cordonnier*, of Havre, saved from a boat	19
1918	Oct.	1	Schooner *Atlantico*, of Oporto, saved from a boat	6
			do. second service, saved from a second boat	3

PENZANCE—NEWLYN—PENLEE

THE FIRST BOAT designed solely for lifesaving (as distinct from conversions of other types of craft) was the *Original*, built by a ship's carpenter, Henry Greathead, of Shields, in 1789, under the auspices of a committee of gentlemen at Shields who had been much concerned by the tragic loss of life from ships wrecked at the mouth of the Tyne. Greathead had been one of the entrants in a competition for a self-righting lifeboat sponsored by this committee, and the *Original* was based partly on a model submitted by William Wouldhave, which won half the prize of two guineas, and partly on plans put forward by members of the committee itself. However, this lifeboat did not include Wouldhave's self-righting principle, probably because of the extra weight involved, but she incorporated Greathead's own idea of a curved keel. The *Original* was a 30 ft. ten oared, double-ended boat, and she remained in use in the vicinity of Shields for forty years. The success she achieved in rescuing shipwrecked crews led to her being adopted as the prototype for thirty other lifeboats, all built by Greathead, Lloyd's voting the sum of £2,000 to aid the good work. In 1803 one of these boats was stationed at Penzance, in Mount's Bay, its cost being defrayed by a generous grant from Lloyd's, and a liberally supported local fund.

This represented the first attempt to create an organised lifeboat station in the Duchy, and details of the manner of its formation were published in the *Royal Cornwall Gazette*, of October 29th:—

"Penzance, October 21st 1803.—Whereas several Wrecks happened last winter in the Mount's-Bay, and many lives were unfortunately lost; on representation of which to the Committee at Lloyd's, they have liberally contributed the sum of FIFTY POUNDS towards the purchase of a LIFE-BOAT for the said Bay, the full cost of which will be about ONE HUNDRED AND FIFTY POUNDS. The Inhabitants thereof, and of Cornwall in general are requested to contribute towards carrying this laudable undertaking into effect; for which purpose Subscriptions are received at the PENZANCE, FALMOUTH and HELSTON BANKS, and at the CORNISH BANK, TRURO. The aftermentioned sums are already subscribed:

	£	s.
Committee at Lloyd's	50	0
Messrs. Batten and Son Penzance	5	5
Mr. James Pascoe, Penzance	3	3
George John, Penzance	3	3
L. C. Daubuz	5	5
Mr. Oxnam, Penzance	5	5
Captain Bass, H.M.S. Gannet	5	5
Mr. William Carne, Penzance	5	5
Messrs. Bolitho & Sons, Chyandbur	3	3

Later issues of the paper gave the names of further subscribers to the scheme, these being:

	£	s.
Francis Gregor, Esq., M.P.	5	5
Lord Falmouth	10	10
John Tremenheere	1	1
Thos. Pascoe, Esq., Penzance	3	3
William J. G. Nicholls, Esq., Trereife	5	5
John Scobell, Esq., of Nance-Alverne	2	2
Cornish Copper Company	5	5
George C. Fox and Sons	5	5
Wood & Cornish	3	3
Rev. Theo Robyns	1	1
Rev. W. Oxnam	1	1
Lord de Dunstanville	10	0
Rev. Wm. Borlase	2	2
John Rogers, Esq., Penrose	5	0
Wm. Hill, Esq., Penzance	3	3
Henry P. Tremenheere, Esq., Penzance	1	1
Thomas John, Esq., Penzance	1	1
Samuel John, Esq., Penzance	1	1
Rose Price	5	5
R. & J. Cunnack	3	3
Captain Carlyon	1	1
Captain Giddy	1	1

Unquestionably, there was great need for a lifeboat at Penzance. In addition to the growing number of vessels trading to the port, many ships bound up or down Channel sought shelter in Mount's Bay during stormy weather. With northerly or westerly winds, the roadstead was a safe one, but when these shifted to south or east, such craft could soon find themselves in dire peril, surrounded by shallows, rocks and breakers on a dead lee shore, the apparent haven suddenly transformed into a death-trap. Shipwrecks, in consequence, were of frequent occurrence, and the accompanying loss of lives of tragic proportions.

The Penzance of 1803, though a much smaller place than today, had already achieved some distinction as a social and cultural centre. Here, only a few years before, the young Humphry Davy had received his early medical training—Davy, the scientific genius, whose safety-lamp was destined to prove a lifesaving invention of equal merit to the lifeboat itself. Those local gentlemen who subscribed to the purchase of one of Greathead's boats were acting fully in accordance with the enlightened liberal traditions of the town. Cornwall may well honour the memory of these noble-minded pioneers, for they helped to lay the foundations of that great humanitarian service whose work still goes forward today.

Just how long ago it was when this first Cornish lifeboat stood waiting to put off to the rescue of shipwrecked seamen is graphically illustrated by the fact that on October 22nd 1805—the day after the battle of Trafalgar—when Penzance was visited by "a most tremendous gale", she is stated to have been "kept in a state of readiness in case of accident". Among the vessels which put in for shelter during this storm was the ship *Magdalene*, of and for Greenock, from Grenada, with sugar, which had been captured off Cape Clear three weeks previously by the *Vengeador*, Spanish schooner privateer. The *Magdalene* was later recaptured by the frigate *Iris*, which also took a Spanish ship privateer. The *Magdalene* entered Penzance in distress, whilst the Spanish ship, seen off the Bay that same day, was supposed to have been driven by the gale into the North Channel.[1].

The first Penzance lifeboat lasted just under nine years. In an advertisement dated July 1st 1812, she was offered for sale with "all materials compleat for immediate use". This notice also stated that she rowed ten oars, measured 27 feet in length by 10 wide, that her cost had been "upwards of one hundred and seventy pounds", and that she had "never been used". A news item published in the *West Briton* of December 27th that year (kindly furnished by its present Editor, Mr. Claude Berry) described the sale as follows: "We learn that the Life-boat, which several years ago cost 150 guineas, though it has never been used, was on Monday last taken in distress for rent, and sold for 20 guineas. The boat was purchased by subscription. Perhaps the Gentlemen of Penzance and its neighbourhood feel themselves so burthened by providing the poor with provisions at this season that they have nothing to spare for redeeming the Life-boat." The fact that this boat had never been used may probably be attributed to the dislike which was apparent in most shore communities away from the east coast of the Greathead design, for the same thing occurred in several other places.

Despite this failure—if any true pioneering effort may be so described—the people of Penzance were again the first in Cornwall to give public support to the Royal National Institution for the Preservation of Life from Shipwreck when that body was established in 1824. At a meeting held on May 19th, it was decided to form a local Branch of the Institution, and shortly after this (apparently in 1826) the Institution forwarded a lifeboat of the "Plenty" type with launching carriage to Penzance, where Manby's apparatus had already been established (under the Coastguard and Coast Blockade) at least as early as 1825. The Northumberland Report of 1851 says this lifeboat was "wrecked",

1 *Sherborne Mercury*, October 28th 1805.

without specifying when. It continued to figure in the Institution's annual *Reports* down to March 1827, but as lists of stations were omitted from this publication in subsequent years evidence is lacking to show when the boat went out of existence.[1]

Irrespective of the date when the Penzance station again became inoperative, the work of life-saving went on by other means. On the morning of May 24th 1828, the brig *Albion*, of Plymouth, coal laden, was driven on the beach eastward of Newlyn during a heavy S.S.E. gale. She came on shore stern foremost about 200 fathoms from the beach, and the sea, making a clean breach over her, carried away the bulwarks, exposing her crew to the utmost danger. Mr. Richard Pearce, Lloyd's agent, promptly brought Manby's apparatus and one of his own six-oared gigs to the scene; the gig was launched and reached the brig in time to save the master, who had been washed overboard, and was sinking. The crew of five were then rescued from the vessel and landed in a state of great exhaustion, the brig breaking up soon afterwards.

Another gallant rescue by shore boat took place in December 1848. Of some hundred vessels sheltering in Mullion Roads, more than half ran for shelter in Penzance harbour when a S.S.E. gale forced them all from their anchorages. Much damage was caused by collisions when entering the pier in such numbers and so closely together. On Christmas Day, with the wind moderating and westering, two of them (both schooners of Plymouth) hauled out of the pier and made sail. They proved unable to double the Lizard, the wind round to S.S.E., and so were forced to bear up, but it blew too hard with a heavy sea. Failing to reach the pier again, the schooners anchored, but their cables soon broke. The *Kitty* tried to stand to eastward, but most of her canvas was blown away, and she went on shore half-way between Penzance and St. Michael's Mount, where she soon became a total wreck. The crew were taken off by a shore boat at daybreak, except for the boy who was drowned when the foremast went over the side. The second schooner *Stephen Knight* went ashore half-a-mile east of the pier, the crew saving themselves in their own boat.

Steps for providing a new lifeboat at Penzance were taken in 1852, when a boat of the Peake type, measuring 30 ft. by 8 ft. was ordered for the station. The *West Briton* of October 14th 1853 stated that this had

1. Some sources say the lifeboat disappeared in 1828, but this date may have been inferred simply from the fact that Penzance *and all other stations* ceased to be listed in the annual *Reports* during that year.

been built principally through the exertions of Mr. R. Pearce, adding that "steps will be taken to obtain an efficient crew, that the efforts of the Shipwrecked Mariners Society may not be rendered abortive". The cost came to £150, met by the Council, whilst the boat was said to have been built from a plan furnished by Messrs. Semmens and Thomas, of Penzance, who were also, apparently, the builders.[1]. Presumably it was based on a design they had previously entered for the 1851 lifeboat competition organised by the Duke of Northumberland.

A new boathouse was built for the lifeboat in 1856 at a cost of £88. It must have been from this house that she made her only known service launch to the schooner *Hopewell*, of Goole, in distress near Penzance in a gale on October 7th 1858, but rendered no assistance.

This lifeboat was superseded by a new one measuring 30 ft. by 7 ft., and rowing six oars, built by Forrestt of Limehouse to the Peake plan in 1860. She received the name of *Alexandra*[2]. at a most interesting double christening ceremony held at Penzance on March 10th 1863, when that town celebrated the marriage of the Prince and Princess of Wales (later Edward VII and Queen Alexandra). The other boat featured on this occasion was the *Duke of Cornwall*, a surf lifeboat based on the Trinity Works at Penzance, and intended for the use of workmen then engaged in building the Wolf Rock lighthouse.[3]. The *Alexandra*, described as "a picture of strength and brightness, with her crew all equipped for a struggle with the mighty main", was drawn from the lifeboat house on the Western Green to the Eastern Green, and thence up Market Jew Street in procession to church, accompanied by a band, artillery volunteers, coastguards, Naval Reserve, and the *Duke of Cornwall* lifeboat. The naming ceremony was performed on the Green, the boat afterwards being launched.

The *Alexandra*'s only known service took place on January 29th 1865, when she launched to the assistance of the brig *Willie Ridley*, of Plymouth, and it was a most gallant one. During a severe southerly gale the brig dragged her anchors a considerable distance, until she came within a cable's length of the reef off Western Beach. In the absence of the Coxswain, Capt. Fellowes took command of the lifeboat, which

1. The *Life-Boat* (January 1st 1854) states that this boat had been stationed at Penzance by the National Shipwreck Institution, aided by local subscriptions.
2. Or *Princess Alexandra*. Both names are used indiscriminately in the *Cornish Telegraph* of the period.
3. This lighthouse was prepared at Trinity Yard, Old Quay, Penzance, for erection on the Wolf Rock. Work commenced in 1861, and was completed in 1869.

The coaster Falmouth Castle *(407 tons) beached near Porthcurno after she had struck the Lee Ore Reef, off Land's End, March 17th 1919 (Photo: Gibson)*

One of the crew coming ashore by breeches-buoy from the s.s. City of Cardiff *wrecked at Nanjizal Bay, Land's End, March 21st 1912. Although all passengers and crew were saved, the ship became a total loss (Photo: Gibson)*

All sail still aloft, the ship Granite State, *of Portsmouth (New Hampshire), ashore at Porthcurno, in 1895 (Photo: Gibson)*

Salvage work proceeding on the s.s. Cragoswald, *stranded on the Low Lee Rock, near Mousehole, April 29th 1911. Earlier, her crew had been taken off by the Newlyn lifeboat (Photo: Gibson)*

Six Cornish lifeboats racing in Mount's Bay, September 1867 *(see page 117)* *The winners Sennen Cove, with oars aloft, are followed home by the lifeboats from Penzance, Hayle, St Ives, Mullion and Porthleven (From an engraving in the Illustrated London News, September 21st 1867)*

The Penzance lifeboat Dora *launching to the brigantine* Jeune Hortense *on the Eastern Green, Mount's Bay, May 17th 1888*

The brigantine Henry Harvey, *of Hayle, stranded in a gale on Battery Rocks, Mount's Bay, March 25th 1898. Those aboard her were saved by the Penzance lifeboat (Photo: Gibson)*

Sightseers walk out over the sands at low tide to the wreck of the Norwegian barque Petrellen, *the day after she had driven ashore midway between Marazion and Penzance in January 1885 (Photo: Gibson)*

was launched from Wherry Cove, and her crew tried to pull her off through the passage near Lariggan Rocks, but the force of the sea broke four or five oars and drove the lifeboat back broadside on to the beach. Spare oars were obtained, and another attempt made, but again the boat was thrown back broadside on to the rocks. Nothing daunted, the crew took the lifeboat on its carriage to Newlyn and launched there. After hard rowing they reached the brig and threw a hand grapnel on board. The Captain and crew, fearing to stay on the vessel in a perilous position with rising wind and sea, and night coming on, left by way of the main boom and were landed on the beach. During the night the wind moderated, and next day the crew were put back, and proceeded on voyage. For this meritorious rescue Capt. T. H. Fellowes, R.N., Inspecting Commander of the Coastguard at Penzance, was awarded the Silver Medal of the R.N.L.I.

During the following month it was reported that a new lifeboat had been forwarded to Penzance to replace the *Alexandra*, named *Richard Lewis* after the Secretary of the Institution. This lifeboat, the best known of all those stationed at Penzance, achieved a glorious record of services, some of which are among the classics of lifeboat history.

Her first service launch took place on November 22nd 1865, when she put off to the brig *Rhederenden*, of Porsgrund, in a heavy westerly gale, but her assistance was not required. She carried out her first rescue on November 24th 1865, when the brigantine *Tobaco*, of Hamburg (180 tons), bound from Mexico for Hamburg, with logwood, drove ashore on Marazion beach in tremendous seas. News of her plight reached Penzance at daylight that morning, and the *Richard Lewis* was taken on its carriage to the scene. It was then full tide, and on arrival they found the seas making a clean breach over the vessel; her bulwarks had gone and she appeared to be nearly gutted. The crew had taken refuge in the rigging, from where one of the men had fallen, to be seen no more. The *Richard Lewis* was launched with difficulty through the great run of the tide, and after much exertion reached the brigantine, being nearly thrown into her bows by one sea. She successfully grappled with the vessel and took off her crew of five. They broke an oar in landing, but the boat was seized by watchers on shore and hauled up the beach amid tremendous cheers.

On January 11th 1866 the lifeboat was drawn by a team of eight horses to Hayle to help the St. Ives lifeboat save the crew of nine of the stranded s.s. *Bessie* of Hayle. The long struggle of both lifeboat crews to reach the wreck and their coolness and judgement in the actual rescue were described at the time as "beyond all praise".

A year later (on January 5th 1867) the lifeboat rescued the crews of three schooners wrecked near Penzance during an E.S.E. gale and very heavy sea. Soon after daybreak signals of distress were seen off Long Rock, the lifeboat being at once taken towards Marazion. The lifeboatmen found the *Salome* (owned in Brixham but registered at Dartmouth) fast drifting towards the shore. They saved the crew of five men and a boy, and soon after the schooner struck and went to pieces. During the evening, which was intensely dark with very heavy rain, the wind rose to hurricane force and a fearful sea raged in the Bay. Soon after nightfall the schooner *Selina Ann*, of Fowey (115 tons), with coal for Plymouth, fired lights for assistance. The *Richard Lewis* was again drawn by a team of horses towards Marazion, and put off to her, guided by one of the Marazion coastguards who knew the local rocks and shoals, and by the aid of lights which the *Selina Ann* was able to show, the master and crew of four were safely landed. A three-masted schooner, the *Heiress* (105 tons), from Llanelly to London, with coal, had carried away her jib stay and was in imminent danger at the same place. The lifeboat had great difficulty in reaching the vessel, and after battling with the waves for some time, she succeeded in bringing ashore the master and crew of five, making a total of 17 men rescued by the *Richard Lewis* that day. Both the *Salome* and *Selina Ann* went to pieces after their crews had been taken off.

Just two days after these wrecks, the ship *John Gray*, of Glasgow, drove ashore at Long Rock during another tremendous S.E. gale, soon after six o'clock in the evening. The lifeboat was launched into one of the most tremendous seas ever remembered there, and after a dangerous pull, succeeded in reaching the vessel. Thirteen of the nineteen men on board were taken off, although another six remained on their ship till morning. The scene as the *Richard Lewis* returned to the beach was an exciting one. From the bow of the lifeboat shone a borrowed railway signal lamp, her own having been previously damaged on service, whilst behind her loomed the masts of the stranded ship. Eager hands waited on the beach to help heave up the boat. Before morning, the seas broke the *John Gray* into fragments, scattering her cargo of coconuts, rum and sugar along the beach, the six sailors who had refused to leave being drowned. These casualties must be attributed entirely to the obstinacy of the Captain, who is said to have threatened to shoot any of his crew who made use of a rocket line which was also fired on board in an attempt to save them.

On March 17th 1867, the brig *Secret*, of Guernsey (188 tons), from Teignmouth to Swansea in ballast, anchored and signalled for assistance between St. Michael's Mount and Penzance during a S.S.E. gale. The *Richard Lewis* placed a pilot and one of her own crew on board, by whose help the *Secret* was brought safely into Penzance harbour. When landing amid the broken water, however, the lifeboat shipped several seas, one of which carried a lifeboatman overboard, but he reached the shore safely.

A notable event in Cornish lifeboat history took place at Penzance on September 10th 1867, during celebrations held to mark the opening of the new Public Buildings in that town. Four lifeboats decked with ribbons, evergreens and flowers, mounted on their carriages with their crews in cork jackets were drawn through the streets in procession by fine teams of horses, these being the *Richard Lewis*, of Penzance, the *Moses* of St. Ives, the *Isis* of Hayle, and the new Mullion boat, *Daniel J. Draper*, which was christened and launched that same day. These boats, together with the *Cousins William and Mary Ann of Bideford* of Sennen, and the *Agar Robartes*, of Porthleven, later participated in a rowing contest, won after a hard-fought race by the Sennen entrant, the *Richard Lewis* and *Isis* coming second and third respectively.[1] This occasion was also marked by the opening of a new timber lifeboat-house on the foreshore near the junction of Alexandra Road with the Promenade.

The *Richard Lewis*'s most notable service took place on December 6th 1868. At two o'clock that Sunday afternoon, during a fearful S.S.W. gale, a horseman galloped into Penzance with news of a large vessel in peril in the Bay. The four-oared pilot gig *May Girl* left the harbour to help, but was driven back, while the large eight-oared barge of Sir Edward St. Aubyn, of St. Michael's Mount, which also put out, had to return. When, shortly after, a large barque was seen through the mist to drive ashore between the Mount and Long Rock, the lifeboat, which had been put in a state of readiness, was taken by road to the Eastern Green and launched from the nearby beach with the help of many willing volunteers who went in up to their necks to get her afloat. Unfortunately, the Captain had seen the gig and barge put back, but failed to observe the lifeboat, and so ordered his own boats out. The first was immediately upset and stove against the side

1. During a subsequent contest of this kind, held in September 1869, a free fight developed between the crews of the *Moses* and *Richard Lewis* when rounding the Gear Pole, enabling the Sennen men to make another comfortable win.

of the wreck. The jolly boat, measuring 22ft. by 6ft., was then launched, and the Captain with about nine of his crew got into her. They made for the shore, but after covering half the distance a breaker turned the boat over. Three of them seized the keel, and though three times driven from their hold, they reached the shallows. William Jeffery, the champion wrestler of the West, a skilled boatman and a strong swimmer, threw off his coat and plunged into the surf, grasping three men one by one and handing them to other people behind him. Two others reached the shore, but one died a few minutes later. The other five men who had been in the boat were drowned.

The lifeboat was launched to windward through a tremendous ground sea, and it took the crew a pull of over an hour to reach the barque. As they were pulling under her stern, however, a great sea capsized the boat and threw all in her into the water. Coxswain Thomas Carbis, veteran of many heroic rescues, became jammed by wreckage under the boat and nearly lost his life, having to dive several times to extricate himself. He was dragged aboard apparently dead and landed in this state. Hodge, who pulled stroke oar, was washed away, and the crew had not strength enough to pull towards him, but he, too, was eventually recovered.

It was thought advisable to have a fresh crew, for a second trip, which, led by W. Blackmore, Chief Officer of Coastguard, as Coxswain, included also Samuel Higgs, Jun., French Vice Consul. The lifeboat had to be pulled to windward in the face of tremendous sea and wind. Sometimes she was thrown almost vertical by the waves, and the onlookers thought she must go over. She was pushed forward inch by inch and at last, during a temporary lull, the remaining eight on the wreck were pulled aboard and safely landed. Ten minutes after the rescue the masts went, and in half an hour the vessel was in fragments. She was the barque *North Britain*, of Southampton (703 tons register), carrying 950 tons of timber from Quebec. Five Silver Medals were awarded in connection with this most gallant service (to Capt. R. B. Cay, R.N., W. Blackmore, Coastguard, S. Higgs, jun., Coxswain T. Carbis, and Second Coxswain Higgins, Coastguard, the last two being Second Service Clasps). Thanks on Vellum went to N. B. Downing, Esq., Hon. Sec.; G. Desreaux and William Jeffery.

The *Richard Lewis* performed a remarkable overland journey on the night of January 30th 1869, when she was drawn for nine miles over roads, some broken up and others flooded, to the wreck of the barque *Choice* of Shields, at Praa Sands, performing this terrible journey in under two hours. Eight of the barque's crew were saved by rocket apparatus, three others being drowned. The *Choice* was bound with rye from Sulina (Rumania) for Falmouth, for orders.

A fate unique in the annals of shipping befell the brig *Otto*, of Moss, which during a southerly gale on January 26th 1873, drove ashore on the Eastern Green, for of her it may truthfully be said that she was wrecked in a bay of treacle in the middle of a submerged forest! She came in during the night, and after an unsuccessful attempt had been made to reach her by rocket, the lifeboat was brought to the scene and launched with great difficulty in the face of a terrific sea. Whilst approaching the wreck, the lifeboat completely severed a trunk of one of the ancient trees which in earlier times formed part of a wood surrounding St. Michael's Mount. The storms of the preceding winter had laid bare some remains of this old forest, which now formed a minor hazard to shipping. All eight members of the *Otto's* crew were safely rescued and landed, together with a dog and a pig. As the tide receded, the brig was left lying in a little "dock", in which much of her cargo of sugar dissolved, forming the "treacle" to which allusion has been made! To show their appreciation of this service, the Norwegian Government decreed by Royal resolution the Silver Medal for Civic Deeds (Borgerdaad) to Nicholas B. Downing, Swedish and Norwegian Vice Consul at Penzance and Hon. Sec. of the lifeboat branch; Captain W. Howarth, R.N., Inspecting Commander of Coastguard; and William Blackmore, Chief Officer of Coastguard at Penzance. A few days after this (on February 2nd) the *Richard Lewis* saved the crew of four from the schooner *Marie Emilie*, of Lorient. The lifeboat was twice driven back by heavy rollers, and had seven oars broken. At the wreck, she was twice hurled by breakers on to the vessel's deck, but at the third attempt succeeded in her mission.

On the morning of May 17th 1879 a mounted messenger entered Penzance with the news that a brig was ashore at Perran, five miles to the east. A strong southerly wind with heavy seas prevailed at the time. The Marazion rocket apparatus was taken to the scene and fired several rockets over the brig, which lay 5-600 yards from the shore, but owing to the crew's ignorance of their use, only one man was saved by this means. A barge manned by young fishermen from St. Michael's Mount got alongside, but the crew refused to leave. The *Richard Lewis* had meantime come alongside, but no notice was taken of her, the master being unwilling to let the crew leave, although the brig—the *Ponthieu*, of Vannes, from Pomaron for Liverpool with iron ore—was in a most dangerous position among breakers, and encompassed by rocks. The lifeboat stood by for some time, and eventually the five members of the crew got into her, but the master refused to leave. He seemed to have no sense of danger, and as the wind increased and his ship began to break up around him, he remained coolly unperturbed, and for most of the time kept his back turned contemptuously on the shouting crowd ashore.

The lifeboat returned to the brig and again urged him to leave, but he persisted in his refusal, and so, as she had sustained three broken oars in the heavy seas, they returned to Penzance and landed the rescued men. Commissioned Boatman Gould, of the Coastguard, then volunteered to go to the wreck along the line with a letter from the French Vice Consul urging the Captain to leave, but received only a refusal for his pains, and nearly lost his life in the attempt. The vessel was now disintegrating, and Capt. Kergulant became trapped in the debris when her masts went over the side. The watchers thought he must be lost; but the amazing and indestructible man reappeared eventually among the wreckage, and seated himself on the mainyard! A second rocket was now fired, and Capt. Kergulant at last allowed himself to be drawn ashore by breeches buoy. A great sea caused him to lose his hold when 30 yards from shore, but this foolhardy yet fortunate man was snatched from the waves by the coastguards who formed a human chain. On landing, he refused a drink of brandy, saying he was already full of salt water, and also ignored the doctor's advice that he should go to bed! The French Government awarded a Gold Medal to Gould and sent its thanks to the lifeboat crew.

On February 14th 1881 the lifeboat assisted to save the ship *Macduff*, of Glasgow, in difficulties off Lamorna in a strong S.S.W. wind; and on September 5th of the same year saved the barquentine *Neilly*, of Bridgwater in a S.E. gale, together with her crew of six. A third vessel saved that year was the barque *Pampero*, of Swansea, which, with a crew of 14, had been disabled and was in a dangerous position on the evening of November 24th, this task being performed in conjunction with the salvage vessel *Queen of the Bay*.

On February 11th 1885 an entirely new lifeboat station was opened at Penzance. A new boathouse, with bell turret, had been erected on a more convenient site granted by the Town Council in the harbour at the foot of Jennings' Lane, the cost of the building together with a new lifeboat and carriage, being met by a gift of £1,000 from Henry Martin

Harvey, Esq., of Launceston.[1]. The boat itself (named the *Dora*) was first launched at Lariggan on March 6th 1884, with great success; and at the official inauguration of the station in the following year she was drawn through the town to the house, where the donor handed the key to Commander C. la Primaudaye, R.N., Inspector of Lifeboats. The boat was subsequently launched from the quay into the harbour, a distance of ten feet, launching being normally effected by carriage down the slip opposite Abbey Steps.

The *Dora*'s first service took place on January 31st 1885, when, in

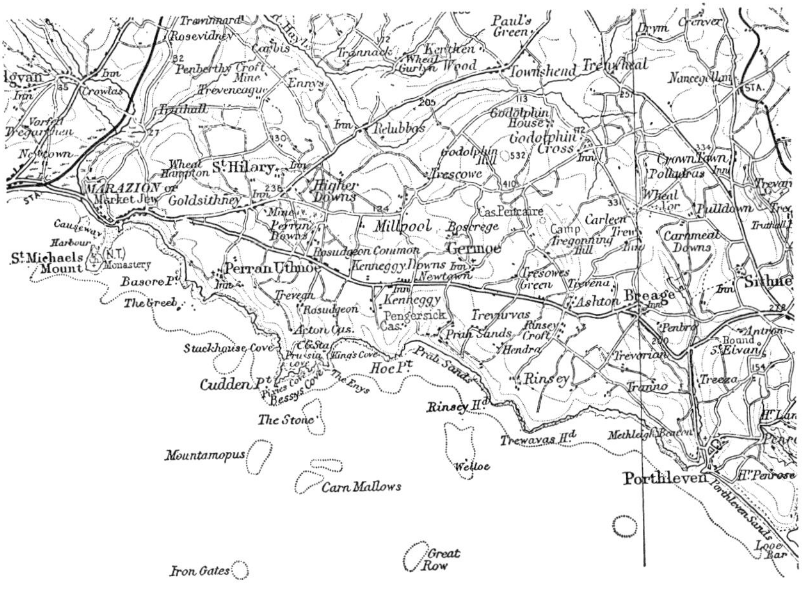

answer to signals of distress from the barque *Petrellen*, of Porsgrund, riding heavily at her anchors in a strong S.S.W. gale, she was launched at 7.30 a.m. The crew, being afraid the vessel would go ashore, jumped into the lifeboat as soon as she came alongside, but the master and mate remained on board. Next morning, the weather having moderated, the crew returned to the *Petrellen*, but at 9.30 p.m. the wind and sea again increased, her cables parted, and she drove ashore between Penzance and Marazion. The *Dora* landed the whole crew of ten at

1. The house itself cost £575-6s.-6d., and was sold to Penzance Corporation in 1917 for £200. It is still in existence.

about 11.30, the barque herself becoming a total wreck. A vessel of 335 tons, she was bound from Garlieston for Porsgrund in ballast.

The *Dora* performed a double rescue during the early morning of December 8th 1886, saving four of the crew of the dandy *Alliance* and five and a dog from the schooner *Golden Light*, both of Penzance, shortly before they drove ashore near Ponsandane river. On May 17th following she rescued three men and a boy from the brigantine *Jeune Hortense*, of Nantes, which, bound from Brest for Fowey in ballast, dragged her anchors in a heavy ground sea and stranded on the Eastern Green. Also that same year (on November 8th) she landed the crew of five from the three-masted schooner *Livingstone*, from Swansea for London with coal, which brought up inside the Gear Pole just clear of the Frenchman Rock after failing to reach Penzance pierhead during a strong S.E. gale.

The *Dora* subsequently performed several more valuable services, before being replaced by a new lifeboat, the *Elizabeth and Blanche*, in 1895. Larger than her predecessor, this boat rowed twelve oars, double banked, and among her services, two are worth mentioning, particularly as they concerned well-known Cornish vessels. On February 25th 1898, during a westerly gale, the schooner *Mary James*, of Penzance, parted her cable when being taken to the floating dock, and being light, she immediately drifted out of the harbour towards the Cressar Reef, about 400 fathoms distant. The lifeboat reached her just as she brought up to two anchors about 50 fathoms short of the reef. The lifeboat took off and landed her crew of ten; but two hours later the wind shifted to the north and decreased, enabling the schooner to be taken into the harbour. Exactly a month later the lifeboat launched to assist the brigantine *Henry Harvey*, of Hayle, from Runcorn with coal, which had missed stays in trying to make harbour in a strong N.E. gale. She dropped anchor, but the cable parted, and the vessel struck near the Battery Rocks, becoming a total wreck. The *Elizabeth and Blanche* saved her crew of four, together with a woman passenger.

A second lifeboat bearing this name was placed at Penzance in 1899. Her first service took place on March 29th 1901, when she landed the master and crew of eight from the barque *Antarctic*, of Swansea, homeward bound from London in ballast, which had become dangerously embayed in Mount's Bay. The vessel was later saved.

In 1908 the *Elizabeth and Blanche* was transferred to Newlyn harbour to simplify launching, this being the first move towards the establishment of the present Penlee station. The Penzance station was not immediately closed, however, a smaller self-righting rowing boat, the *Cape of Good Hope*, being placed there in case of accident or necessity. Her first service took place on February 21st 1909, when the steam drifter *Renown*, of Yarmouth, with a crew of nine, failing to make Penzance Pier in a fresh breeze and rough sea, grounded about a cable's length from the pier head. Being damaged and unmanageable thereafter, she drove ashore about 200 yards east of the Albert Pier. With great difficulty the lifeboat took a wire rope to the pier head, where it was grasped by hundreds of willing hands, and she was hauled off and berthed by the lifeboat crew in the harbour.

The *Cape of Good Hope* was eventually damaged on service; and all attempts at repairing her having failed, the Coxswain, Mr. Will Nicholls, was invited to visit the Poplar depot, where he selected a sailing boat as replacement from twenty lying there. Named *Janet Hoyle*, she had been built in 1896, being formerly stationed at Ayr, and was a lovely craft. Writing of his experiences in her, Mr. Nicholls states[1]: "My most arduous lifeboat service took place in 1912. On Boxing Day, at 8 a.m., the Coastguard called at my house in Penzance. He brought a message to the effect that a steamer was drifting disabled across the Bay. Neither the Sennen nor Newlyn boats could go out, and so the message was passed to me. A strong gale (90 m.p.h.) was then raging; shop fronts at Penzance were blown in and boats overturned in the harbour, Penzance Pier Head being under water. At 8.30 the boat was in the water, all reefs taken in, and away. I have often since thought of the appearance of the Bay when I rounded the pier head. The seas were pitiless, and the first one aboard completely filled the boat. I remember thinking that this was my last trip! I thrashed out about eight miles, opening up all the Western land, and then, seeing nothing of the ship, came about, and edged towards Porthleven, where the broken sea was worse. I was from there signalled by green rocket to 'recall.'

The vessel—the s.s. *Tripolitania*—had gone ashore on Loe Bar; and, to judge the height of the seas, she was thrown at dead low water to twenty feet above high water. She remained there for years until broken up for scrap. There were only two lifeboats afloat on that day, my own, and the Plymouth boat, which was blown ashore in Jennycliff Bay inside the breakwater. The stemhead of my boat was split from the planking, and the lovely paintwork smashed in spots into the drab first coat. She looked like a spotted leopard. Two of my men died on the

1. In a letter, dated September 1959, to Mr. D. C. Vosper, Saltash.

following Thursday from pneumonia, which shows the terrible conditions we had to face on that service."

The Penzance station was closed in 1917. Meanwhile, at Newlyn, the *Elizabeth and Blanche* had been doing some good work. A large, heavy Watson boat, not particularly suited to long carriage journeys, like her predecessors, but intended for operations over a greater range of sea and coast, she was kept on her carriage at the water's edge just outside the Old Harbour arm. Her most notable service occurred on December 28th 1908. The ship *Clan MacPherson*, of Glasgow, in tow, had anchored, windbound, the previous evening in Mount's Bay, it then blowing very strong from the north. Early next morning the wind flew to S.E., and during the day increased to a gale. The ship and tug got under weigh, but made very slow progress, and at 2.30 p.m. when close inshore off Mousehole Island the tow rope parted. The lifeboat crew, who had been standing by, immediately launched, but before they reached the scene the tug had connected again. However, in the gale and with the flood setting in, both ship and tug were carried across the Bay towards the eastern shore. The lifeboat intercepted them, and on the Coxswain's advice they let go their anchors.

Just then the schooner *Titania*, of Salcombe was seen running into the Bay before the gale. The lifeboat went to her, and piloted the vessel safely into Newlyn harbour, arriving at 4.30 p.m. They then returned to the *Clan MacPherson*, and as the weather had much worsened, with hail and snow, the master decided to abandon ship. The lifeboat landed the whole crew of twenty at Newlyn, arriving at 7 p.m. Fortunately, the ship's cables held, and the men returned to her next day, the sea having considerably moderated.

On April 29th 1911, the steamer *Cragoswald*, of Newcastle, whilst bound from Barry to Venice with coal, and carrying 27 hands, stranded on the Low Lee Rock in fine weather. The *Elizabeth and Blanche* stood by the vessel for three hours and at the Captain's request landed the engineer, who was ill. She then returned to the ship, remaining in attendance until 5 p.m. At this time the steamer foundered, all the men on board being rescued by the lifeboat.

At the height of an exceptionally heavy gale on the morning of December 13th 1911, the barque *Saluto*, of Christiansand, entered the Bay from the westward, her situation appearing very dangerous amid the tremendous seas. The lifeboat, with a fair wind, caught up with the vessel which was driving rapidly eastward before the gale, and took off her entire crew of 13 when she was within half-a-mile of the Grebe

Rocks off Perran. This rescue was performed with great difficulty and danger, as the barque was rolling heavily, four oars being broken. She was bound from England for Barbados in ballast, and later became a total wreck.

Just eight days later, at 11.30 a.m. a large steamship was observed on her beam ends trying to work into the Bay in a S.W. gale and very heavy ground seas. The steam trawler *Labore et Honore* was standing by her but the lifeboat was launched and reached her just after she had anchored. She proved to be the *Hellopes*, of Liverpool, and was sinking, twelve of her crew having already been taken off by the trawler. The lifeboat saved the master, mate and two engineers, the steamer immediately afterwards sinking in twenty fathoms.

The last service rendered by the *Elizabeth and Blanche* whilst stationed at Newlyn took place on March 13th 1912, when she stood by the London steamer *South America*, from Hamburg for Cardiff in ballast, which had run ashore at Merthen Point. The crew landed in their own boats, but just before the lifeboat's arrival some had returned on board. There was a moderate W.S.W. gale, and the lifeboat remained in attendance for more than eleven hours in case of necessity.

The decision to form a station at Penlee had been taken as early as 1910, a house with direct slipway at this headland half-way between Newlyn and Mousehole being regarded as the best answer to local launching problems. The necessary shore establishment was built in 1912-3 at a cost of £2,850, the *Elizabeth and Blanche* being transferred from Newlyn in the latter year. Alterations and enlargements have been made from time to time to suit the motor lifeboats stationed there since 1922.

The first launch at Penlee took place on October 22nd 1914 when, shortly after ten p.m. the lifeboat went to the assistance of the s.s. *Liguria*, of Genoa, for Swansea in ballast, which had lost her propeller. She made communication between the *Liguria* and another steamer, which then towed the disabled vessel to safety.

The Penlee boat performed a very gallant service on November 4th-5th 1918 when the Admiralty tug *Epic* stranded about a mile from shore at Long Rock in very heavy seas. She was launched at 8.30 p.m. on the 4th, and on reaching the scene found broken water a long way outside the tug, making it highly dangerous to approach. The lifeboat stood by some hours until the rocket apparatus had fired a line aboard, and then returned to base. It was later reported, however, that the crew had not been saved by this means, and the *Elizabeth and Blanche* again proceeded to Long Rock. The sea now having moderated somewhat she got alongside at the third attempt and took off the tug's crew of 17. The grapnel rope was then cut, and the lifeboat manoeuvred out of a most dangerous situation. Five men had got ashore before her arrival, four of them by means of a raft.

The last service performed by the *Elizabeth and Blanche* at this station proved to be a most arduous one. The s.s. *Concordia*, of Genoa lost her propeller S.W. of the Wolf Light, and the lifeboat put off at 3.30 p.m. on July 8th 1922, in a whole S.W. gale and very heavy seas, under reefed canvas, arriving on the scene at 7 p.m. A steamer was also standing by, and on the advice of Coxswain Blewett she anchored. Tugs had also been sent for, and so after a while the lifeboat returned. The motor lifeboat from St. Mary's set off for the *Concordia*, but after three hours' running had an engine failure, and the weather making it impossible to open the hatches to effect repairs, she sailed to Falmouth, arriving at 6 a.m. after being 14½ hours at sea. The Penlee boat returned to Mousehole, where she was then stationed during alterations to Penlee slipway, at 10.45 p.m. The *Concordia* was later brought to Falmouth with the help of the s.s. *Uskmouth*, of Newport. Extra monetary awards were granted to the Penlee crew, with a Letter of Thanks to Coxswain Blewett in recognition of their strenuous efforts on this occasion.

The *Elizabeth and Blanche* was replaced by this station's first motor lifeboat *The Brothers* on December 20th 1922. She was of the Watson type, and the first to be fitted with the new 90 B.H.P. 6-cylinder engine. Her donors were the Misses Eddy of Torquay, who also defrayed the cost of alterations to the house and slipway made necessary by the larger boat.

The Brothers had a fine opportunity of proving her excellent qualities during her first service, on January 3rd-4th 1923. She launched at 1.45p.m. on the 3rd to the assistance of the s.s. *Dubravka*, of Dubrovnik, which had anchored in a strong westerly gale after losing her propeller. A passing steamship had been engaged to help, but before communication could be made, the *Dubravka* dragged her anchors to within 20 yards of the Runnelstone rocks. She was in great danger, as it was getting dark and the gale worsening. The steamer dropped another anchor and held while a tug, which had arrived, tried towing, but all the wire ropes parted. The lifeboat then took off 27 of the 31 on board the *Dubravka*, coming in so near the rocks to effect this rescue that the waves were breaking over her. Another steamship tried to tow without success, and the lifeboat left for Newlyn, arriving at 11.30 p.m. Early next morning she returned to the Runnelstone, but found the *Dubravka* had been towed to Falmouth.

The Brothers received another call to the Runnelstone on October 8th of that same year, when the s.s. *City of Westminster*, of Liverpool, from Belfast for Rotterdam with 73 on board, struck on these dreaded rocks in thick weather. The Sennen Cove lifeboat arrived at 11 a.m. and took off three women and ten of the crew, whilst the Penlee boat took on board a number of the crew who had left in their own boats, and then went alongside to take off the officers. The steamer was rolling heavily in the ground swell, making the operation a very difficult one. The Penlee boat saved 35, the remaining 25 being towed to port in their own boats by the Penzance steam drifter *Pioneer*. During the night the steamship's siren was sounding, so both lifeboats went off again, only to find the operating lanyard had been fouled in the rigging. She eventually became a total wreck.

The second motor lifeboat at Penlee, named *W. & S.*, was dedicated by the Vicar of Paul during an inaugural ceremony held on August 15th 1931. The initials of the boat's name were chosen by the donors, Winifred Alice Coode and Sidney Webb.

This boat was first called out on service only a few weeks afterwards, when the steamship *Opal*, of Glasgow, bound from Antwerp for Cardiff with maize, shifted her cargo in heavy seas, causing a dangerous list. The crew took to the lifeboats, which were repeatedly swamped, one, with six men, capsizing three times. Both the Master and Chief Engineer were drowned, the former being washed from the bridge. The coasting steamer *Wild Rose* threw lifebelts to the crew and eventually picked them all up, the men later being handed over to Newlyn pilots in Mount's Bay. After the fisheries patrol ship H.M.S. *Spey* had wirelessed information to Land's End, both the Penlee and Sennen Cove lifeboats launched and made for the scene. The Captain's body was recovered by the *W. & S.* at 10.30 p.m. The *Opal* herself foundered three miles S.W. of the Longships.

The *W. & S.* performed a splendid service on January 27th 1936 when she rescued the crew of the s.s. *Taycraig*, of London (163 tons: owned by the County of Cornwall Shipping Co., Redruth). At 2.15 a.m. a coastguard message gave warning of a ship apparently on fire near Gear Rock. The lifeboat made her way in a strong S.S.W. gale and heavy rain to the casualty, which she reached in half-an-hour. With the aid of her searchlight she discovered that the vessel was not on fire, but partially submerged, with the crew of nine on the fo'csle head, the blaze having been caused by a mattress burnt to attract attention. She had struck the rock in a heavy swell, and was wedged by the stern, the wreck lying end on to the gale giving no lee for shelter. The Coxswain managed to bring his boat along the starboard side of the fo'csle and threw a grappling iron aboard. The lifeboat was flung violently about, so that the *Taycraig's* master expected her to be thrown on his deck, but the Coxswain kept her off with only minor damage. Choosing the right moment, seven of the crew jumped one by one into the lifeboat, then one landed on the neck of the Bowman and the ninth fell into the sea, but was at once seized and dragged on board. The lifeboat then made for Penzance, arriving at 3.25. What made this service all the more remarkable was the fact that one of the two 40 h.p. engines of the lifeboat had not been working. Coxswain Frank Blewett was awarded the R.N.L.I.'s Bronze Medal for the bold and skilful manner in which the rescue had been performed. The *Taycraig* was light, and bound for Newlyn to load stone, when the sudden southerly gale drove her on to the rocks.

A very curious incident took place during the early morning of January 21st 1939, when an Ostend trawler, the *Paul Therese*, broke from her moorings in Newlyn Harbour and drifted to sea, her crew of six being asleep and unconscious of any danger. There was a southerly gale, with rough sea and thick weather. After the Coastguard had reported the mishap, the *W. & S.* launched at 4.35 a.m. and found the trawler near the rocks between Penzance and St. Michael's Mount. A lifeboatman boarded her and roused the crew, and the lifeboat towed her from danger. Her crew then started the engine and she followed the lifeboat into clear water.

At 10.15 p.m. on February 21st 1940, it was reported that a vessel had gone ashore near the Penzer Rocks, the weather being foggy with a southerly wind and moderate sea. The *W. & S.* found the s.s. *Westown*, of London, at anchor, she having managed to get off the shore by the time the lifeboat arrived. The *W. & S.* then escorted her into Newlyn. Five days before this steamer had been in difficulties in Gerrans Bay, and was then escorted to safety by the Falmouth lifeboat.

This station performed a number of services to casualties during the Second World War. The first of these was on September 1st 1940, when a minesweeper (the *Royalo*, a former Grimsby trawler) blew up off Penzance harbour. The Penlee boat launched to give assistance, but the survivors were picked up by small boats. On March 8th 1941 she brought ashore three wounded men and a body from the s.s. *Margo*, of Cardiff, which had anchored in the Bay, then put a doctor on board to attend to another severely wounded man, and finally brought the latter and the Captain ashore.

A remarkable occurrence took place on December 18th 1944, when a German submarine struck the Wolf Rock and sank. The *W. & S.* and naval vessels went to the rescue; the latter picked up a number of survivors, but none were rescued by the Penlee boat.

An arduous service in bitter weather and heavy seas was carried out on January 3rd 1945. The British steamer *Strait Fisher* capsized off Cape Cornwall, her cargo having shifted in a strong N.W. wind and a very rough sea. The *W. & S.* launched at 4.20 p.m. and reached the scene at 6.15, but found only an empty boat, a naval trawler having picked up ten of the steamer's crew.

At 4.15 p.m. on March 21st 1945, the Penzance coastguards reported that one, and possibly two, vessels required help nine miles west of the Lizard. There was thick fog in the area, with a light southerly wind and smooth sea. At 5.30 the Penlee lifeboat found the American steamer *John R. Park*, of San Francisco, sinking after being torpedoed. Naval ships were standing by, and one of them informed the lifeboat that the whole crew of 76 had been rescued. Some of these had returned to the steamer to recover their kit, and the lifeboat stood by until they had again left her. The Lizard lifeboat *Duke of York* also launched and stood by this casualty.

A most dramatic shipwreck took place at Prussia Cove on April 23rd 1947 when the obsolete battleship *Warspite* on tow from Portsmouth to the Clyde to be broken up parted from her tugs and came ashore right under the cliffs. The Penlee and Lizard lifeboats were first alerted at 4.15 a.m. on the 22nd when *Warspite* and her escorts ran into bad weather twenty miles south of Penlee and fifteen from the Wolf. The crews at both stations assembled, but four hours later the weather moderated, enabling them to stand down. At 1.50 p.m. on the 23rd, however, the coastguard informed Penlee that the warship had again broken away from her tugs and was adrift one mile S.W. of Cudden Point. A strong south westerly gale was then blowing with a rough sea. The *W. & S.* launched ten minutes later and found *Warspite* aground on Mount Malpas Ledge. With some difficulty in the heavy seas, the lifeboat came in close enough for the Coxswain, Mr. Edwin Madron, to hail her by megaphone. It was now dead low water, and he told her master that with the rising tide she would be in greater danger, as she would be floated off and drift ashore. He advised the master to abandon ship, but the latter refused, believing that it was impossible to board the lifeboat in such seas.

The *W. & S.* now made for Newlyn harbour, as she could not be hauled up her slipway in the prevailing conditions, arriving there at 4.15. At 5.30 she put out a second time when it was learned that *Warspite* had indeed been driven off the ledge and seemed likely to come ashore, as Coxswain Madron had predicted. The gale had increased and the sea was very rough, the boat taking three-quarters of an hour to reach Cudden Point. She found *Warspite* ashore just east of Prussia Cove, her bow head to the wind and seas, fo'csle awash and seas breaking around "B" turret. Coxswain Madron took the lifeboat to windward of the wreck, turned, and with the gale behind, approached her bows.

Thirty foot waves were now crashing down on the warship and all around lay heavy broken water. Her starboard side was close to shore, whilst off her port side and at her stern rocks appeared and disappeared in the breaking seas, but between the battleship and the rocks was a channel forty yards wide

Into this channel Coxswain Madron took the lifeboat, pumping oil as he went, with rocks both to starboard and ahead. The space was too narrow for the normal practice of anchoring to windward and veering down, so they were obliged to get alongside, despite the danger. He could have found some shelter under the stern, but a boat slung in davits outboard made this impossible. Choosing a spot at the far end of the quarter deck, he turned in the narrow channel and brought the boat near the battleship head to wind, and during a momentary lull threw two lines on board.

They now had the perilous task of keeping the lifeboat in close enough for the men to jump into her. So great was the rise and fall of the seas that the lifeboatmen were sometimes looking down on *Warspite's* deck whilst next moment the boat was in great danger of being smashed against the bulge near her water line.

Watching each sea, the Coxswain went full speed ahead to meet it, and then full speed astern. For 35 minutes he kept manoeuvring in this way, and whenever the lifeboat swung close enough he called on the men to jump in turn. Seven jumped as soon as they were called, but the eighth took a long time before venturing the leap. Throughout this time the two mechanics were crouched under the canopy at the controls, unable to see what was going on, but knowing that the slightest delay

The Norwegian barque Saluto *(826 tons) drifting shorewards near Perranuthnoe, December 13th 1911, after her crew had been taken off by the Newlyn lifeboat* Elizabeth and Blanche

The barque Noisiel, *of Nantes, ashore at Praa Sands, in 1905 (Photo: Gibson)*

Spray shrouds the s.s. Tripolitania *as she lies broadside to the waves on the great shingle bank of Loe Bar, Porthleven, December 26th 1912 She had been bound for Barry in ballast and the force of the gale drove her relentlessly eastward across Mount's Bay. The Captain's decision to beach her here saved nearly all his crew, although the vessel was flung far above the tideline by the enormous seas and all attempts to salve her failed (Photo: Gibson)*

in carrying out the Coxswain's instructions would mean disaster for all. The lifeboat returned to Newlyn Harbour with the rescued crew at 7.45 that evening.

For this truly classic rescue Coxswain Edwin F. Madron was awarded the Silver Medal; Mechanic John H. Drew the Bronze Medal; whilst the other members of the crew—Joseph J. Madron, 2nd Coxswain, John T. Worth, Bowman, J. C. Wallis, Ass. Mechanic, A. Madron, B. Jeffery and C. Williams—received the Institution's Thanks on Vellum. This was Edwin Madron's first service as Coxswain; and to him was presented also the "Maud Smith" reward for the bravest lifeboat deed of the year. *Warspite* was later got off the rocks and beached on the sands of St. Michael's Mount, where for some time her huge bulk remained whilst she was slowly broken up for scrap. On July 15th 1950, the trawler *Barnet*, used as a maid-of-all-work by the salvage company attempting to tow *Warspite* from the rocks, became holed when tied up to the wreck for the night. On casting off, her engine room was found to be flooded. The Admiralty tug *Freebooter* came alongside and began to pump the water out, but it could not be controlled. *Freebooter* accordingly removed those on board, and *Barnet* was allowed to drift ashore. When the Penlee reserve lifeboat *M.O.Y.E.* reached the scene she was requested to land the rescued men at Newlyn. The *M.O.Y.E.* also stood by the tug *Masterman*, of Falmouth, engaged for the *Warspite* salvage operation, which struck the Hogus Rocks near Marazion on November 11th 1950, in a full S.W. gale and heavy seas. Her sister tug *Tradesman* also received damage whilst trying to tow her. *Masterman* was repaired with a cement box, whilst *Tradesman* had to be towed to Falmouth by the tug *Superman*.

In conjunction with Land's End Radio, the local hospitals commenced, at the end of the war, a highly successful medical advice service, which in 1951 was extended to the regular reception of casualties taken from calling ships. Many of the cases of boarding doctors and landing patients have been accomplished by the Penlee lifeboats, the first of these services taking place on January 27th 1951 and many similar missions have since been undertaken by the Penlee station, as a glance at the Service Record will show.

A French trawler, the *Vert Prairial*, of Dieppe, was wrecked at Wireless Point, Porthcurno, on March 14th 1956. The *W. & S.* accordingly launched at 7.15 a.m. in a rough sea with fresh S.E. wind, and found the trawler on her beam ends among the rocks. There was no sign of life, but several bodies were floating in the surf. The lifeboat picked up two and the rest were washed ashore, to be recovered by the coastguard, the whole crew of 17 having been drowned. The *Vert Prairial* had left Brixham for the west on the previous day. The steamer *Peninnis* heard an S.O.S. from her, but this was the last message received from the unfortunate trawler.

When the 827-ton s.s. *Yewcroft*, bound from Cliffe for Bristol with cement, ran aground near Cudden Point in dense fog during the evening of July 8th 1956, the Penlee reserve lifeboat *Millie Walton* which launched to her assistance was herself stranded on the rocks near St. Michael's Mount. When she ran on the rocks, her plight was seen by several boatmen who took an anchor out from the lifeboat to use as a kedge to pull herself clear, and the lifeboat at once proceeded to the wreck.

When the *Yewcroft* grounded her bow and stern were on the rocks, with nothing under the midship section, and as the tide receded, the weight of the cargo broke her back. This occurred two hours after she had gone ashore, the vessel folding like a jack-knife. Coxswain Madron, who was aboard her at the time, said that "she went off like a gun". Most of the crew were on the forward section when this occurred. Others who were still aft jumped the gap and joined the lifeboat which was alongside. The Chief Engineer, however, was unable to make the jump, but he was saved by a rocket line fired by an L.S.A. crew which had previously been made fast there. The *Yewcroft* was first seen running through the fog towards Trevean Beach by a local resident, who hurried to the cliffs and tried to warn the crew of their danger, but they could not hear his voice. He then made telephone calls for assistance from a nearby house which brought the lifeboat and L.S.A. to the scene. The steamer was so completely lost that in her first distress call, at 5.46 p.m., she stated herself to be "hard aground forward, position unknown, but think near Brissons".

On September 17th 1960 Lady Tedder performed the naming ceremony of the present Penlee lifeboat *Solomon Browne*. This was provided out of three legacies and the general funds of the R.N.L.I., the chief donor concerned being Miss Lydia Mary Dyer Browne of Launceston. This magnificent boat is of the 47-ft Watson type fitted with two 60 h.p. diesel engines, and cost £35,000. She is equipped with radio telephony (including VHF for communication with Service helicopters), radio direction finder, echo sounder, loud hailer, searchlight, signal lamp and rocket throwing pistol, and has an enclosed wheelhouse. Her top speed is nine knots, and she carries sufficient fuel for 270 miles. The boat is kept on a hydraulically-operated cradle in the boathouse, this being tilted to allow her to run down the slipway, which is now the steepest in use in this country.

A most unfortunate accident occurred to this lifeboat on December 30th 1961, when being rehoused after landing a sick man from the tanker *Varicella* at Newlyn. The *Solomon Browne* arrived back on station at 6.30 p.m., and as she was about to be hauled up the keelway of the slip a heavy sea carried her broadside to the north for about ten feet, pulling the winch wire with her. Two of the shore helpers were struck on the legs, one fell into the water with several ribs broken; whilst the other was knocked on to the rocks and into the sea, being dead when recovered. At the inquest it was stated that the two gentlemen were aged 72 and 78 respectively, but the honorary medical adviser confirmed that they were extremely fit and capable. As a result of this accident, it was decided by the local branch to adopt new regulations regarding the employment of helpers aged 65 or over.

When the trawler *Jeanne Gougy* ran ashore on the Armed Knight off Land's End on November 3rd 1962, the *Solomon Browne* joined the Sennen boat in searching for survivors. The two lifeboats also joined in an attempted rescue operation when the 682-ton Spanish coaster *Juan Ferrer* ran ashore and capsized near Lamorna in the early hours of October 23rd 1963. Her master had time only to send out one distress call shortly before 3 a.m., "Aground in the vicinity of Land's End", before she turned over, the inrush of water putting her generator out of action and leaving her without lights or radio, quite invisible from the shore, and unable to indicate her position.

The Coastguards marshalled their rescue team in the car park at Land's End and made an intensive search along the cliffs from Lamorna round Land's End to Cape Cornwall, a distance of ten miles. It was at Boscawen Point, near Lamorna, that a party of watchers saw, with the aid of their torches, the *Juan Ferrer's* captain clinging to wreckage in the water, and were able to direct the *Solomon Browne* to his rescue. About a mile further west, another party found three survivors walking along a farm lane. In addition to the two lifeboats, the Dutch salvage tug *Titan*, the Fishery Protection vessel H.M.S. *Watchful* and the Trinity House vessel *Stella* also joined in the search, whilst three helicopters hovered over the sea area. One of these recovered two bodies. Under the helicopters' direction the lifeboats and other craft picked up several other bodies. Four only were saved alive out of the Spanish vessel's crew of fifteen.

Laden with general cargo, the *Juan Ferrer* had encountered fog at 11.20 p.m. on the 22nd, and struck the rocks at 2.50 a.m. the following morning. An attempt made to launch the ship's port boat failed, as it was smashed against the side of the ship, whilst the starboard lifeboat could not be used because the rocks were against that side of the ship, and she was heeled over to port. The master stayed on board until she went down, and then swam away without a lifejacket, being in the water four hours before being picked up. The other survivors had lifejackets, and after struggling ashore remained on the rocks for an hour before climbing to the cliff-top. The coaster appeared to have struck the rocks head on, for there was a big hole in her bows extending from the water line to her keel.

This tragic shipwreck focussed public attention on the dangerous, unprotected stretch of coastline between Mousehole and Land's End, where, during the previous fifteen years, thirty-nine seamen were said to have lost their lives. In January 1964 it was announced that Trinity House had decided to place a light and fog signal at Tater-du, just beyond Carn Boscawen, and near the spot where the unfortunate Spanish vessel had run ashore.

BOAT RECORD, PENZANCE

Years on Station	Length, Breadth, Depth	Type, Oars, Crew	Weight, Cost, O. No.	Built, Year, Builder	Boat's Name, Donor, Authority
1803- 1812	27′ 10′	NC 10	 £150	1803 Hy. Great-head, S. Shields	— Lloyd's & local subscribers Town Council
1826-		Plenty		1826	— Nat. Shipwreck Instn. N.S.I.
1853- 1860	30′ 8′ 3′ 8″	Peake 10	1t15 £150	1853 Semmens & Thomas, Penzance	— N.S.I. & local subscribers N.S.I.
1860- 1865	30′ 7′ 3′ 3″	Peake 6	1t10 £153 —	1860 Forrestt, Limehouse	*Alexandra*[1] R.N.L.I. R.N.L.I.
1865- 1884	32′ 7′ 4″ 3′ 6″	SR 10 13	 £210	1865	*Richard Lewis* J. Chamberlain, Birmingham R.N.L.I.

1884- 1895	34′ 8′	SR 10 13	 £363 49	1884 Woolfe, Shadwell	*Dora* H. M. Harvey, Hexworthy R.N.L.I.
1895- 1899	36′ 8′ 3″	SR 12 15	 £310 378	1895 Watermans, Cremyll	*Elizabeth and Blanche* Misses Smitheman, Albury R.N.L.I.
1899- 1908	38′ 9′ 6″	W 12 15	5t £753 424	1899 Chambers & Colby	*Elizabeth and Blanche* Misses Smitheman, Albury R.N.L.I.
1908- 1912	34′ 7′ 6″	SR 10 13	3t11 £423 341	1892[2] Forrestt, Wivenhoe	*Cape of Good Hope* Leg. Chas. Hawkins, London R.N.L.I.
1912- 1917	34′ 8′ 3″	SR 10 13	3t3 £334 386	1896[3] Woolfe, Shadwell	*Janet Hoyle* T. K. Hardie, London R.N.L.I.

1 Given this name in 1863. She was sometimes referred to as the *Princess Alexandra*
2 Formerly stationed at Runswick, Yorkshire.
3 Formerly stationed at Ayr.

BOAT RECORD, NEWLYN

Years on Station	Length, Breadth, Depth	Type, Oars, Crew	Weight, Cost, O. No.	Built, Year, Builder	Boat's Name Donor, Authority
1908- 1913	38′ 12′ 6″	W 12 15	5t £753 424	1899[1] Chambers & Colby,	*Elizabeth and Blanche* Misses Smitheman, Albury R.N.L.I.

1 Formerly stationed at Penzance, later at Penlee.

BOAT RECORD, PENLEE

Years on Station	Length, Breadth, Depth	Type, Oars, Crew	Weight, Cost, O. No.	Built, Year, Builder	Boat's Name Donor, Authority
1913- 1922	38′ 12′ 6″	W 12 15	5t £753 424	1899[1] Chambers & Colby,	*Elizabeth and Blanche* Misses Smitheman, Albury R.N.L.I.
1922- 1931	45′ 12′ 6″	W(M) — 8	16t15 £13214 671	1922 J. S. White, E. Cowes	*The Brothers* Misses Eddy, Torquay R.N.L.I.
1931- 1960	45′ 6″ 12′ 6″	WC(M) — 8	19t12 £7684 736	1931 J. S. White, Cowes	*W. & S.* Legs. Miss Coode, Launceston, & Miss Young, R.N.L.I. [Twickenham
1960-	47′ 13′	W(M) — 8	22t14 £35500 954	1960 Wm. Osborne Ltd., Little- hampton	*Solomon Browne* Miss Browne, Launceston, etc. R.N.L.I.

1 At Penzance 1899-1908; at Newlyn 1908-13.

SERVICE RECORD, PENZANCE

Alexandra Lifeboat

1865	Jan.	29	Brig *Willie Ridley*, of Plymouth, saved	8

Richard Lewis Lifeboat

1865	Nov.	24	Brigantine *Tobaco*, of Hamburg, saved	5
		25	Unknown vessel, no service	
1866	Jan.	11	s.s. *Bessie*, of Hayle, saved	5
1867	Jan.	5	Schooner *Salome*, of Dartmouth, saved	6
			Brigantine *Selina Ann*, of Fowey, saved	5
			Schooner *Heiress*, of Teignmouth, saved	6
		7	Ship *John Gray*, of Glasgow, saved	13
	Mar.	17	Brig *Secret*, of Guernsey, placed pilot on board	
1868	Dec.	6	Barque *North Britain*, of Southampton, saved	8
1873	Jan.	26	Brig *Otto*, of Moss, saved	8
	Feb.	2	Schooner *Marie Emilie*, of Lorient, saved	4
1879	May	17	Brig *Ponthieu*, of Vannes, saved	5
1881	Feb.	14	Ship *Macduff*, of Glasgow, assisted to save vessel	
	Sept.	5	Barquentine *Neilly*, of Bridgwater, assisted to save vessel and	6
	Nov.	24-5	Barque *Pampero*, of Swansea, assisted to save vessel and	14

Dora Lifeboat

1885	Jan.	31	Barque *Petrellen*, of Porsgrund, saved	8
	Feb.	1	do. saved	10
	Apr.	24	Fishing boats of Penzance } stood by and gave warning of obstruction	
		25	do.	
1886	Dec.	8	Dandy *Alliance*, of Penzance, saved	4
			Schooner *Golden Light*, of Penzance, saved	5
1888	May	17	Brigantine *Jeune Hortense*, of Nantes, saved	4
	Nov.	8	Schooner *Livingstone*, of Lancaster, saved	5
1889	Jan.	29	Trawler *Blue Bell*, of Plymouth, saved	4
1890	Dec.	31	Brig. *Dorothy*, of North Shields, assisted to save vessel and	8
1891	Mar.	10	Schooner *Joseph Nicholson*, of Newcastle, saved vessel and	5
1892	Oct.	15	Schooner *Express*, of Dublin, saved vessel and	4

Elizabeth and Blanche (I) Lifeboat

1896	Dec.	8	Saved a man blown from the sea wall	1
1897	Mar.	4	Barque *Lady Gladys*, of Tonsberg, saved	17
1898	Feb.	25	Schooner *Mary James*, of Penzance, saved	10
	Mar.	25	Brigantine *Henry Harvey*, of Hayle, saved	6

Elizabeth and Blanche (II) Lifeboat

1901	Mar.	29	Barque *Antarctic*, of Swansea, landed 9	
	Dec.	23	Brigantine *St. Joseph*, of Lannion, assisted to save vessel	
1907	Sept.	27	s.s. *Ellesmere*, of Manchester, took doctor to steamer	

Cape of Good Hope Lifeboat

1909	Feb.	21	Steam drifter *Renown*, of Yarmouth, saved vessel and	9

Janet Hoyle Lifeboat

1912	Dec.	26	s.s. *Tripolitania*, of Genoa, no service	
1913	Mar.	21	Steam and sailing trawlers entering harbour, stood by	

SERVICE RECORD, NEWLYN

Elizabeth and Blanche Lifeboat

1908	Dec.	28	Ship *Clan MacPherson*, of Glasgow, saved	20
			Schooner *Titania*, of Salcombe, rendered assistance	
1910	Feb.	19	Ketch Trawler *Radiance*, of Brixham, stood by	
	Oct.	14	Schooner *Lizzie*, of Weymouth, stood by	
1911	Jan.	12-13	Schooner *Lizzie Ellen*, of Cardigan, helped vessel to safety	
	Apr.	29	s.s. *Cragoswald*, of Newcastle, saved	27
	Oct.	13	s.s. *Hammershus*, of Copenhagen, assisted to save vessel	
	Dec.	13	Barque *Saluto*, of Christiansand, saved	13
		21	s.s. *Hellopes*, of Liverpool, saved	4
1912	Feb.	11	Barque *Etoile Polaire*, of Fécamp, saved vessel and	8
		28-29	s.s. *Northlands*, of Cardiff, stood by and assisted to save vessel	
	Mar.	13	s.s. *South America*, of London, stood by	

SERVICE RECORD, PENLEE

Elizabeth and Blanche Lifeboat

1914	Oct.	22	s.s. *Liguria*, of Genoa, assisted to save vessel	
1915	Oct.	27-28	Ketch *Traly*, of Tralee, assisted to save vessel and	6
1917	Apr.	11	s.s. *West Wales*, of Cardiff, assisted to save vessel	
1918	Nov.	4	H.M. Tug *Epic*, stood by	
		5	do. saved	17
1922	Jan.	24	s.s. *Gracefield*, of Swansea, stood by	
	July	8	s.s. *Concordia*, of Genoa, stood by	

The Brothers Lifeboat

1923	Jan.	3	s.s. *Dubravka*, of Dubrovnik, saved	27
	Sept.	30	s.s. *Nicolas Norbert*, of Boulogne, stood by and piloted to Newlyn	
	Oct.	8	s.s. *City of Westminster*, of Liverpool, saved	35
1924	Aug.	5	s.s. *River Ely*, of Cardiff, rendered assistance and landed 5	
1925	Sept.	29	Steam Trawler *Rig*, of Ramsgate, saved vessel	
1928	Oct.	27	s.s. *Mona*, of Antwerp, escorted vessel to safety	

W. & S. Lifeboat

1931	Sept.	5	s.s. *Opal*, of Glasgow, recovered a body	
1935	Nov.	30	Motor fishing boat *Adventure*, of Penzance, saved boat and	5
	Dec.	8	s.s. *Cornish Rose*, of Liverpool, assisted to save vessel and	9
1936	Jan.	27	s.s. *Taycraig*, of London, saved	9
	June	19	Motor fishing boat *Gleaner*, of Penzance, escorted boat to safety	
1937	Jan.	11	Motor Trawler *Vierge Marie*, (0.332), of Ostend, picked up 2 bodies and saved	1
	Oct.	20	Motor fishing boat *Apapa*, of Newlyn, saved boat and	1
1938	Apr.	22	Steam fishing boat *Pioneer*, of Penzance, towed in boat and saved	2
1939	Jan.	31	Motor Trawler *Paul Therese*, of Ostend, saved vessel and	6
1940	Feb.	7	Motor Trawler *Jeannine*, of Ostend, escorted vessel to safety	
		21	s.s. *Westown*, of London, escorted to harbour	

B.A.S.P. (Reserve) Lifeboat

1940	Mar.	17	s.s. *Miervaldis*, of Riga, gave help	

W. and S. Lifeboat

1941	Feb.	2-3	s.s. *Heire*, of Oslo, stood by	
	Mar.	8	s.s. *Margo*, of Cardiff, first service, landed 3 and 1 body	
			do. second service, landed 2	
			do. third service, rendered assistance	
			s.s. *Falkvik*, of Solvesborg, landed 1 wounded man	
1942	Apr.	24	Fishing boats *Margaret*, *Boy Don* and *Alsace Lorraine*, of Newlyn, saved three boats and	12
1943	Aug.	20	Dutch motor vessel, stood by	
1944	Jan.	6	s.s. *Solstad*, of Norrkoping, saved	14
1945	Jan.	3	s.s. *Strait Fisher*, of Cardiff, saved empty boat	
	Mar.	21	s.s. *John R. Park*, of San Francisco, stood by	
		26	m.v. *Pacific*, of Groningen, saved ship's boat	
		29	H.M.C.S. *Teme*, (K.458), landed 57	
	Dec.	18	Yacht *Diane*, of Cowes, saved yacht and	7
1947	Apr.	23	Obsolete warship, *Warspite*, saved	8
1948	Feb.	7	Wolf Rock Lighthouse, stood by while supplies were dropped	
	June	7	Landed the bodies of 2 bathers	
1949	Sept.	4	Customs motor launch *Badger*, stood by while towed to harbour	
		19	Sea Otter Seaplane, stood by	

M.O.Y.E. (Reserve) Lifeboat

1950	July	15	Salvage vessel *Barnet*, landed 5 from tug *Freebooter*	
	Nov.	11	Tug *Masterman*, of Falmouth, stood by	

W. and S. Lifeboat

1951	Jan.	27	Post Office cable ship *Ariel*, landed a sick man and 2 doctors	
1952	Oct.	25	Seven Stones Light-vessel, landed a keeper	
1955	Oct.	13	s.s. *Manolito*, of Puerto Limon, landed an injured man	
1956	Mar.	1	m.v. *Crete Avon*, of London, stood by and gave help	
		14	Trawler *Vert Prairial*, (D.1517), of Dieppe, picked up 2 bodies	

Millie Walton (Reserve) Lifeboat

1956	July	8	s.s. *Yewcroft*, of Glasgow, saved	10

W. and S. Lifeboat

1956	Nov.	6	s.s. *Pontoporos*, of Piraeus, took out a doctor saving a life	1
	Dec.	9	m.v. *Harborough*, of London, landed an injured man	
1957	Mar.	10	Recovered a rubber dinghy	
	July	29	S. tanker *Cnosa*, of Monrovia, landed an injured man	
	Sept.	18	s.s. *Alexandria*, landed an injured man	
	Dec.	25	M. tanker *Hemisinus*, of London, landed an injured man	
1958	Aug.	15	Motor fishing vessel *Hesperian*, of Penzance, saved vessel and	6
1959	Feb.	2	s.s. *Asia*, of Liverpool, landed a sick man	1
	Apr.	1	Crabber *Pluie de Roses*, (A.2435), of Audierne, landed 4	
	July	19	s.s. *Lindi*, of Antwerp, landed a sick man	
	Sept.	12	m.v. *San Blas*, of Stockholm, landed an injured man	1
		23	Tanker *London Resolution*, of London, landed an injured man	1
1960	Feb.	18	Fishing boat *May*, (SS.47), of St. Ives, saved boat and	1
	May	8	Seven Stones Light-vessel, landed a sick man	1
		19	m.v. *Saarland*, of Vagesack, landed sick man from H.M.S. *Undine*	1
		25	m.v. *Sangara*, of Liverpool, landed sick woman and baby	1
	June	15	m.v. *Rowallan Castle*, of London, landed sick man	

Solomon Browne Lifeboat

1960	Sept.	25	m.v. *Fravizo*, of Amsterdam, landed a woman and baby	
		27	Tanker *Belmare*, of Gothenburg, landed a body	
1961	Jan.	4	m.v. *Mille Heering*, of Copenhagen, landed a sick man	
	Feb.	18	m.v. *Leersum*, of Amsterdam, landed a sick man	
	May	17	s.s. *Olympos*, of Piraeus, landed a sick man	
		25	Fishing boat *Susan*, of Penzance, saved boat and	2
	June	16	m.v. *Doreifs*, of Monrovia, landed sick child	
		25	m.v. *La Colina*, of London, landed injured man	
			s.s. *Mergus*, of Helsingborg, landed sick man	
	Aug.	15	Tanker *Kent*, of London, landed sick man	
	Sept.	15	m.v. *King Charles*, of London, landed sick man	
		24	m.v. *Iron Horse*, of Newcastle, landed sick man	
	Dec.	12	Tanker *Border Falcon*, of Newcastle, landed sick man	
		18	m.v. *Naess Pioneer*, of London, embarked 2 and landed 2, saving	1
		27	s.s. *Okeanis*, of Piraeus, landed sick man	
		30	Tanker *Varicella*, of London, landed sick man	
1962	Mar.	5	s.s. *River Afton*, of Newcastle, landed injured man	
	May	5	Tanker *Haminella*, of London, landed 2 sick men	
	Sept.	1	m.v. *Ben Hope*, of Leith, landed 2 injured men	
		9	m.v. *Uskport*, of Newport, landed a sick man	
	Dec.	3	Tug *Ocean Bull*, of Ostend, landed a sick man	
1963	Feb.	27	m.v. *Livanita*, of Grimstad, landed a sick man	
	Apr.	13	Motor boat *Ranger*, gave help	
	Aug.	21	Troopship *Upshur*, of San Francisco, landed a sick man	
	Oct.	12	s.s. *American Merchant*, of New York, landed a sick man	
		23	m.v. *Juan Ferrer*, of Valencia, landed a body and saved	1
1964	May	7	Fishing boat *Sheila*, of Newlyn, in difficulties at Praa Sands, escorted boat to Newlyn	
		12	Tanker *Haminea*, of London, landed injured master	

5

PORTHLEVEN

THE LITTLE SEAPORT and fishing harbour of Porthleven, on the eastern side of Mount's Bay, lies on a stretch of coastline that has a long and most distinguished connection with the noble work of saving life at sea. One of the earliest examples of this occurred on December 29th 1807, when the frigate H.M.S. *Anson*, forty-four guns, commanded by Capt. Lydiard, was wrecked on Loe Bar. The *Anson* had left Falmouth on Christmas Eve to take up her station off Brest as a look-out ship for the Channel Fleet. On the evening of the 27th, however, a violent storm, blowing about W. of S.W., sprang up; and during the night the *Anson* stood off about W.N.W., the wind then blowing very hard. The following morning she steered for Falmouth, across the entrance of the Channel. During the hours of darkness, however, the ship had run too far to the northward, and consequently when she bore up for Falmouth, instead of having the Lizard on the port side of her course, it was on the starboard. No one on board, of course, knew this at the time.

Land was first sighted about one in the afternoon of the 28th, and the ship immediately put about and steered S.E. by S. About three o'clock they stood in to make land again, which they sighted at four, and recognized to their horror as the Lizard. Capt. Lydiard at once put about again, stood on for half-an-hour, and let go the best bower anchor. They were now hopelessly embayed, and, as the storm continued to rage with terrible violence, the master, to save as many lives as possible, decided to run his vessel on shore.

The *Anson* drove in among the breakers which were crashing with great fury along Loe Bar. The tremendous sea broke over the ship's masts, which soon went by the board, the mainmast forming a kind of floating bridge to the shore, along which many of the crew were able to escape. Capt. Lydiard, who behaved with great gallantry on this occasion, lost his life when endeavouring to extricate a boy entangled below the mast, being three times washed away by heavy seas, the last of which swept him to his death. Mr. Smith, the ship's surgeon, also lost his life in attempting to save his son, who was on board with him.

Hundreds of spectators flocked to the scene of the wreck, and great deeds of heroism were performed by two Cornish Methodist preachers, who crossed from the shore to the ship by means of the fallen mainmast and rescued many people too seriously injured to save themselves. These two men were Mr. Foxwell, of Mullion, a popular local preacher, and Mr. Tobias Roberts, saddler and ironmonger, of Helston. Mr. Foxwell was the first to enter the ship at the head of a party which saved many lives. No one could be seen on the *Anson* when they reached her deck, but going below they found several helpless people, among them two women and two children. Mr. Roberts passed repeatedly from the ship to the shore carrying maimed seamen and one of the women on his back, but the children could not be saved. The ship's stores (which may possibly have included the gold rumoured to have been on board) were placed under Mr. Roberts' charge; and when he was repeatedly assaulted by a gang of plunderers, he seized their ringleader and gave him "a decent threshing". Whether these "execrable wretches" were local wreckers or mutinous members of the crew (for there had previously been trouble of this kind on board) is not clear from contemporary sources.

But if some were saved, a great many others perished. Soon after the *Anson* struck, several seamen took refuge in the round-house, where they became hemmed in by the wreck of the rigging, which fell with the masts. These eventually gained their escape when the ship went to pieces, but only one of them reached the shore alive. Just how many perished altogether was never definitely ascertained, as many of the soldiers on board deserted when reaching the shore; estimates vary from between sixty and a hundred. Capt. Lydiard was buried with full military honours at Falmouth on January 3rd 1808, and the ship's surgeon and a midshipman at Helston. Other victims were bundled in heaps into large pits dug in the cliff above, without any burial rites, this being then the customary practice. Such treatment caused much indignation and as a result, the eminent Cornish M.P. Davies Gilbert framed an Act, passed in June 1808, which required all bodies cast up by the sea to be interred in churchyards and parochial burying-grounds.

Other, even more important, consequences followed from the *Anson* disaster. Among those who had witnessed this terrible wreck was a young man from Helston called Henry Trengrouse. Deeply moved by the dreadful scenes he had witnessed, he gave much thought to the problem of how to bring help to shipwrecked seamen by establishing some kind of communication with them from shore. He eventually devised a form of rocket apparatus for carrying a line to the ship, this invention being far safer and less cumbersome than the shot-and-chain proposed by Lieut. John Bell in 1791, and Capt. Manby's mortar exhibited in February 1807. Trengrouse devoted his life and sacrificed his fortune in the perfecting of his apparatus, and in endeavouring to win Government support for it. Recognition of the merits of his appliance came but slowly, however, and he died in poverty a disappointed man, in 1854.

Yet, even in his lifetime, Trengrouse had the satisfaction of knowing that his apparatus had proved itself in service, and had actually saved lives. His rockets, or "travellers," were employed in connection with a shipwreck near Porthleven, in 1821, by Mr. Roberts, hero of the *Anson* disaster, of which we take the following account from the *Western Luminary*, dated March 13th:

"Last Saturday morning before daylight, the *Peggy*, J. Scotland, master, laden with oranges, ran upon the rocks under a cliff in the vicinity of Porthleven; fortunately the tide had started to ebb, which favoured her remaining whole, so that after about two hours, with the assistance of the people assembled on the shore the crew were enabled to land in safety. Under Mr. Tobias Roberts' agency, great exertions were made to land the cargo, and one of Mr. Trengrouse's invented travellers for conveying persons or property to land in case of shipwreck was made trial of, and found to answer admirably. The advantages this little machine is capable of affording may be surmised from the circumstance of the first four or five cart loads of goods which were cellared, were of those landed from the vessel direct, on the top of the cliff."

In addition to the rocket apparatus, Trengrouse invented the cork jacket, or "life preserver", a device which has been of almost equal value in lifesaving work. He also built a model lifeboat, which though unsinkable, did not possess the self-righting principle. Cornwall, indeed, has every reason to honour the memory of this man who devoted his life and his talents so unsparingly to this noblest of causes.

At the first Committee Meeting of the Lifeboat Institution to decide awards for bravery, held on July 10th 1824, one Gold and three Silver Medals were awarded. Two of the Silver Medals went to William Rowe and John Freeman, of Helston, and cash rewards were given to twenty-four others. They had saved eight persons from a brig wrecked at Halzephron during the previous April, this gallant service being described in the *Royal Cornwall Gazette* of May 1st in the following words: "On Friday last the brig *Olive*, of Tenby, John Williams master, bound from that place to Little Hampton with culm was wrecked near Gunwalloe in Mount's Bay. Providentially the lives of all on board, seven men and a young woman, the sister of the captain, were saved. The vessel came on shore at Halzephron, under a perpendicular cliff upwards of two hundred feet in height, and but for the spirited exertions of some young men of Gunwalloe and Porthleven, who risked their own lives to save those of the sufferers, they must all have perished." According to another source[1], the *Olive* had been driven by a hurricane into Mount's Bay, where she anchored, but the cable soon parting, the vessel grounded near a narrow beach under high cliffs. "A Cornishman" swam out with a line, by which all were brought safely ashore. A year after this, eight seamen "of Helston" were rewarded for helping ashore five sailors in a ship's boat from the South Sea whaler *Phoenix* wrecked at Praa Sands. Eight coastguards, pilots and fishermen were also rewarded for saving six others by boat.

The great dangers and perils constantly run by those who participate in efforts of lifesaving at sea are graphically illustrated by a tragic incident which occurred at Prussia Cove in 1841. The *Mary Stewart*[2], described as "a fine new schooner, of 300 tons burthen," bound from Cardiff to Constantinople with iron, was dismasted on March 18th when about 30 miles to the west of Scilly. The brig *Anne*, of Dartmouth, took her in tow, and brought her into Mount's Bay, but was obliged to abandon the vessel on the night of the 21st, owing to the severity of the weather. Next morning, the *Mary Stewart* was discovered at anchor in a very dangerous situation near Praa Sands. A messenger was at once sent to Penzance to obtain assistance. It was blowing a heavy gale at the time, but as soon as it moderated the *Sylvia* revenue cutter and the trawl-boat *Four Brothers*, of Dartmouth, got under weigh and headed for the spot. In the meantime, however, Lieut. Smith, Chief Officer of the Coastguard at Prussia Cove, had manned his boat, and was attempting to push off; but almost before the men were seated at their oars, the boat capsized, and five of his crew, including a local volunteer, were dashed against the rocks and perished, in sight of their wives and children.

However, although their mission had been a tragic failure, the ship and men they had gone out to aid were saved by other means, for the *Sylvia* and *Four Brothers* succeeded in reaching the *Mary Stewart* and

1. *The West of England Magazine*, Vol. III, No. 31, 1888.
2. *Mary Stuart*, in some accounts.

took off all eleven persons on board. It was not considered prudent to weigh the vessel's anchors, as being so near the shore she would probably have drifted on the rocks before she could be started ahead. On the following day, however, the cutter and trawler returned to the scene, and after great exertions, very skilfully directed, towed her into Gwavas Lake.

The first steps towards the establishing of a lifeboat at Porthleven were taken in 1862, when a Committee Meeting of the R.N.L.I. held on July 31st reported that T. J. Agar Robartes, Esq., was prepared to give £150 for that purpose. In December of the same year an estimate of £145 5s. for building a boathouse on land at Breageside leased from Edward Coode of St. Austell was approved.[1] The first Porthleven lifeboat built by Forrestt of Limehouse in 1863, measured 30ft. in length, and rowed six oars. She underwent a successful trial at the Regent's Canal Dock, Limehouse, on February 26th, and with her carriage subsequently received a free conveyance to Cornwall by rail. After being drawn on her carriage through Helston, she formed part of a procession in that town to celebrate the marriage of the Prince and Princess of Wales on March 10th. The Mayor and Corporation attended church in the morning, accompanied by the whole of the Sunday Schools in the town and the 7th and 18th Rifle Corps, following which the procession re-formed, and was shortly afterwards joined by the new lifeboat in a waggon drawn by six horses, with crew and equipment on board, and a body of about two hundred miners from the Wendron district, the whole extending over a large space of ground.

This lifeboat, named after her donor, *Agar-Robartes*, was not required on service until December 5th 1866, when, with the weather thick and dirty and a strong wind blowing from W.S.W., the Finnish barque *Salmi*, bound from Shields for Civita Vecchia, with coal, was seen in a dangerous position off Porthleven, and apparently making for the land. She had experienced thick weather for some days, and her master had lost his reckoning. The lifeboat launched into a heavy sea and, getting alongside, placed four of her own crew on board, who, at the captain's request, helped to get the barque into Falmouth harbour.

The *Agar-Robartes* was replaced in 1882 by a new 34 ft. ten-oared boat, provided from the legacy of Mrs. Eliza Wright, of Southport, and named *Charles Henry Wright* in memory of her late son. This

1. It stood at the top of Breageside on the coast road to Ashton. The site is now occupied by a house with bay windows just around the corner after coming up the incline from the main road.

lifeboat carried out a strenuous service on October 5th 1886. Between eight and nine in the morning, twenty-five fishing boats left Porthleven harbour, the sea being then comparatively smooth. By 10.30 a.m., however, a heavy ground swell had risen, and a red flag was hoisted to advise the boats to hasten to port. This they lost no time in doing, but on nearing the harbour found there would be great danger in attempting to run in. Orders were at once given to man the lifeboat, and the *Charles Henry Wright* was launched from the western jetty—a drop of about eight or nine feet—almost without a scratch. The lifeboat put to sea, and during the next two hours, amid heavy seas, towed into the harbour eight boats with sixteen men on board, who had been afraid to run for the port without assistance. The lifeboat was undoubtedly the means of saving both life and property on this occasion, as several boats narrowly escaped foundering by being driven on the rocks whilst waiting for her. It was said that the crew had unbounded confidence in the lifeboat, which behaved admirably. Great excitement prevailed as each boat made for the harbour, and the Coastguards were stationed on the Western rocks, wearing belts with lifelines attached, to render assistance, which proved unnecessary, however.

A very similar service to this was carried out on May 18th 1888. On that morning, when a strong breeze had thrown home a heavy swell against the harbour entrance, making access to it a perilous adventure, about half the fishing fleet hove in sight. The booms were accordingly lifted, the lifeboat was launched, and the coastguards again stationed themselves on the Western rocks with cork jackets and lines. The *Charles Henry Wright* stood by until all had reached safety, and towed some boats into the inner basin. Several craft had narrow escapes, notably the *Seek*, which nearly ran ashore.

Launching the Porthleven lifeboats by carriage from the boathouse above the harbour at Breageside had always presented difficulties, and sometimes proved impossible. At low tide and in heavy weather when the inner basin was impounded with a movable breakwater to keep out the ground seas, the booms, as mentioned above, had to be raised to give her egress. There were even times (as in the 1886 service) when the lifeboat had to be pushed over the jetty, with the water a considerable distance from the top of the quay. Because of these unsatisfactory conditions, a new house and slipway launching direct into the harbour on the northern side of the entrance channel were constructed in 1894-5, at a cost of nearly £1,500. Although this new arrangement solved the low-water launching problem, the house suffered great buffeting from the heavy seas, and at such times the boat could not put to sea. A high tide on October 8th 1896, accompanied by a gale and heavy ground sea, broke in the wooden doors of the house and completely filled the lifeboat with water. Had she not been securely fastened down she would have been washed out of the building. New iron barred gates were substituted for the wooden ones, but during a gale in 1906 the roof was badly damaged and the house again flooded.[1]

The last service of the *Charles Henry Wright* took place on December 4th 1898, when the ship *Antonin*, of Dunkirk, which had been trying to beat out of the bay in a strong S.W. breeze, rough sea and thick weather, was seen in a dangerous position. The lifeboat found the ship close to a lee shore, about one and a half miles from Porthleven. On approaching, the Coxswain signalled to the *Antonin* to anchor, and then took ashore a telegram requesting the despatch of tugs from Falmouth. These arrived during the afternoon and the lifeboat went off again to see that the ship got away safely.

A new lifeboat to replace the *Charles Henry Wright* arrived at Porthleven in 1900. Of the self-righting type, she measured 35 ft. in length, rowing ten oars, and was presented by Mrs. Mary Ann White, of London, and named *John Francis White*. Her first call came at the end of that year when, on the evening of December 29th, the barque *Polykarp*, of Grimstad, with coal from Barry for Pernambuco, anchored in distress about a quarter of a mile from shore. She was accompanied by a steamer, which had apparently been trying to tow her to Penzance. In answer to flares from the steamer, the lifeboat put out shortly after nine o'clock. The *Polykarp*, which had sailed on Christmas Eve, encountered a heavy gale which blew her sails almost to ribbons, choked the pumps, and filled her hold with ten feet of water. The master and carpenter came ashore in the lifeboat to make arrangements for a tow to Penzance on the following day. When this was done, the *John Francis White* escorted them there, at the master's request.

The lifeboat herself towed a vessel to safety four years later (on April 3rd 1904). This was the steam launch *Sterry*, of Lowestoft, which, after finding herself unable to steam against a strong westerly wind and high sea, had dropped anchor in a most dangerous position, where she remained for twenty hours, her crew being in an exhausted state and without provisions. The lifeboat put off during the morning, took the *Sterry* in tow, and during the afternoon she was anchored in

1. "When a Life-Boat Was Stationed at Porthleven", F. E. Strike, *The Cornishman*, December 26th 1963.

a safe position. The wind later increased, and but for this help the launch would have sunk. An even finer service was performed by the *John Francis White* on March 17th-18th 1907, when she assisted the Cadgwith lifeboat in saving life from the s.s. *Suevic*, of Liverpool, wrecked at the Lizard. (See Cadgwith station, Vol. III)

During the small hours of May 30th 1907, the Coastguard reported a vessel ashore at Gunwalloe Church Cove, about three miles S.E. of Porthleven. The lifeboat launched in twenty minutes, the weather being moderate but thick, and on arrival found that the vessel—the training brigantine *Polly*, of Bristol, with about fifty on board—had just got clear. At the master's request a lifeboatman went on board to pilot her to Penzance. He said that she had missed stays and struck the ground aft, damaging her rudder. The *Polly* was an ex "fruiter" schooner, built at Brixham, which had been bought in 1875 as a sea-going training vessel attached to the training school housed in the old H.M.S. *Formidable*, at Portishead, and which cruised every year from then until the First World War.

Three months after this the lifeboat launched again after a vessel had been reported ashore on Loe Bar. They found seven men from the casualty rowing towards Porthleven in their own boat but in complete ignorance of their position. They had come from the brigantine *Seiers-krandsen*, of Svendborg, bound for Teignmouth, in ballast. As the weather was very thick, the sailors were taken back to Porthleven at once; but later that evening the Coxswain went back with the Captain to ascertain the exact position of the wreck, and all stood on watch through the night. At five the next morning the lifeboat again went off and helped a Falmouth tug to refloat the brigantine. On Boxing Day, 1912, another casualty occurred on Loe Bar, when the Italian cargo steamer, *Tripolitania*, was driven ashore in a S.W. hurricane. Because of the enormous seas, the *John Francis White* could not launch, but the Penzance lifeboat gallantly put to sea, being recalled, however, before she reached the wreck. Her dreadful experience on that occasion has already been recounted (see page 123). The steamer's crew of twenty-six were saved by the Porthleven rocket apparatus, except for one seaman who, watching his chance as the backwash receded, jumped overboard on to the beach, but was overtaken by the big seas and swept away to his death. So tremendous was the storm that it carried the *Tripolitania* high up on the bar, and all salvage efforts failed to re-launch her. Eventually she was broken up and taken away as scrap.

Porthleven station performed one service during the period of the

First World War. This took place on May 16th 1916, when the s.s. *St. Gothard*, of Glasgow, stranded on the eastern side of the harbour in foggy weather. Her master asked the lifeboat to stand by, and later lifeboatmen went on board when patrol boats connected to help in refloating.

The last lifeboat service ever to be performed at Porthleven occurred on September 30th 1923. Following signals of distress, the *John Francis White* put off in thick fog and found the s.s. *Charbonnier*, of Havre, from Bayonne for Mumbles for orders, with a cargo of pit-props and a crew of thirty. She was in a damaged condition following a collision with another steamer (the *Nicolas-Norbert*, of Boulogne) when about three miles S.W. of Porthleven. The master of the *Charbonnier*, which had a big hole in her side, requested the Coxswain to give him a pilot to Penzance, so the Second Coxswain was put on board, and the lifeboat accompanied them to an anchorage. The *Nicolas-Norbert*, whose bows had been damaged in the collision, was reported by the Coastguard to be showing signals of distress S.S.W. of Cudden Point. The Penlee lifeboat *The Brothers* launched to her aid, and by the time she arrived the fog had cleared a little. The Second Coxswain went on board and piloted the steamship to Newlyn, where the local pilots brought her into harbour.

In 1926 the *John Francis White* was succeeded at Porthleven by *Dash*, a 35 ft. self-righting lifeboat built for the Blyth station in 1902 and which had also served at Brighton. She was then in the reserve fleet. In 1929 it was decided to close the station, the motor lifeboats at the Lizard and Penlee being considered to give sufficient protection to the area.

Porthleven lifeboat station, like many others in Cornwall, is today only a memory, yet some reminders of its work and achievements are still to be seen in the little town. Storms have swept away the old lifeboat slip, but the house of 1894, after suffering some damage, is now employed by a fish-canning firm for keeping shellfish in tanks until required for processing. The original boathouse at Breageside resulted in the name "Lifeboat-terrace" being given to a row of houses built at that site but this name has subsequently been allowed to lapse.

SERVICE RECORD, PORTHLEVEN

Agar-Robartes Lifeboat

1866	Dec.	5	Barque *Salmi* (Russian-Finnish), assisted to save barque and	16

Charles Henry Wright Lifeboat

1886	Oct.	5	Fishing boats, of Porthleven, towed in 8 boats and	16
1888	May	18	Fishing boats, of Porthleven, stood by and towed in some boats	
1898	Dec.	4	Ship *Antonin*, of Dunkirk, brought ashore message for tugs	
			do. (second service) stood by while anchors raised	

John Francis White Lifeboat

1900	Dec.	29	Barque *Polykarp*, of Grimstad, landed 2	
		30	do. stood by while towed to Penzance	
1904	Apr.	3	Steam Launch *Sterry*, of Lowestoft, towed launch to safety	
1907	Mar.	18	s.s. *Suevic*, of Liverpool, saved	18
	May	30	Training Brigantine *Polly*, of Bristol, put pilot on board	
	Aug.	3	Brigantine *Seierskrandsen*, of Svendborg, landed 7 from a boat	
		4	do. assisted to save vessel	
1916	May	16	s.s. *St. Gothard*, of Glasgow, stood by and assisted to save vessel	
1923	Sept.	30	s.s. *Charbonnier*, of Havre, put pilot on board and stood by while towed to Penzance	

BOAT RECORD, PORTHLEVEN

Years on Station	Length, Breadth, Depth	Type, Oars, Crew	Weight, Cost, O. No.	Built, Year, Builder	Boat's Name, Donor, Authority
1863- 1882	30′ 7′ 3′ 3″	SR 6 8	1t10 £200 —	1863 Forrestt, Limehouse	*Agar-Robartes* T. J. Agar Robartes, Esq., R.N.L.I.
1882- 1900	34′ 7′ 9″	SR 10 13	3t10 £363 183	1882[1] Woolfe, Shadwell	*Charles Henry Wright* Leg. Mrs. Eliza Wright, R.N.L.I. [Southport
1900- 1926	35′ 8′ 6″	SR 10 13	3t16 £750 444	1900 Thames Ironworks, Blackwall	*John Francis White* Leg. Mrs. Mary Ann White, R.N.L.I. [London
1926- 1929	35′ 8′ 6″	SR 10 13	3t15 £780 501	1902[2] Thames Ironworks, Blackwall	*Dash* Leg. Miss M. A. Parke, R.N.L.I. [London

1 Altered and improved 1888.
2 Originally stationed at Blyth.

Already published

WRECK AND RESCUE ROUND THE CORNISH COAST

I. The Story of the North Coast Lifeboats:
Bude-Port Isaac-Padstow-Newquay-Hayle

In preparation

III. The Story of the South Coast Lifeboats :
Mullion-The Lizard-Cadgwith-Coverack-Porthoustock-Falmouth-Portloe-Mevagissey-Polkerris-Fowey-Looe